First World War
and Army of Occupation
War Diary
France, Belgium and Germany

23 DIVISION
68 Infantry Brigade
Durham Light Infantry
13th Battalion
17 September 1914 - 31 October 1917

WO95/2182/2

The Naval & Military Press Ltd
www.nmarchive.com
Published in association with The National Archives

Published by

The Naval & Military Press Ltd

Unit 10 Ridgewood Industrial Park,

Uckfield, East Sussex,

TN22 5QE England

Tel: +44 (0) 1825 749494

www.naval-military-press.com

www.nmarchive.com

This diary has been reprinted in facsimile from the original. Any imperfections are inevitably reproduced and the quality may fall short of modern type and cartographic standards.

© **Crown Copyright**
Images reproduced by permission of The National Archives, London, England, 2015.

Contents

Document type	Place/Title	Date From	Date To
Heading	WO95/2187/2 13 Bn Durham Light Inf. Sep 1914-Oct 1917		
Heading	23rd Division 68th Infy Bde 13th Bn Durham Lt Infy Aug 1914-1917 Oct. To Italy.		
Heading	23 Div 68 Bde 13th Battn. Durham Light Infantry. August 1914-August 1915 Went To Western Inf As 12 Battalion In Aug 15		
Heading	23rd Division 13th D.L.I. Vol: I From 24-31.8.15 Aug 18		
War Diary	Bullswater	17/09/1914	23/05/1915
War Diary	Bramshott	08/07/1915	23/08/1915
War Diary	Bullswater	17/09/1914	23/05/1915
War Diary	Bramshott	08/07/1915	23/08/1915
War Diary	Bramshott Camp	24/08/1915	27/08/1915
War Diary	Moule	31/08/1915	31/08/1915
Miscellaneous	Du		
Heading	23rd Division 13th D.L.I. Vol: 2 Sept 15		
War Diary	Moule	01/09/1915	06/09/1915
War Diary	Hazebrouck	07/09/1915	07/09/1915
War Diary	Steenwerck	08/09/1915	09/09/1915
War Diary	Sailly Sur Lys	10/09/1915	17/09/1915
War Diary	Petit-Moulin	18/09/1915	26/09/1915
War Diary	Estaires	27/09/1915	27/09/1915
War Diary	Petit-Moulin	28/09/1915	28/09/1915
War Diary	Estaires	29/09/1915	30/09/1915
Heading	23rd Division 20 Oct Attached 24 Bde Till Nov 2 Only 13th D.L.I. Vol 3 Oct 15		
War Diary	Estaires	01/10/1915	06/10/1915
War Diary	Trenches 55-58	07/10/1915	11/10/1915
War Diary	Erquinghem (South)	12/10/1915	13/10/1915
War Diary	Bois Grenier	14/10/1915	15/10/1915
War Diary	Trenches 55-58	16/10/1915	18/10/1915
War Diary	Jesus Farm	20/10/1915	31/10/1915
Heading	23rd Division 13th D.L.I. Vol: 4 Nov 15		
War Diary	Jesus Farm	01/11/1915	02/11/1915
War Diary	Trenches Near Erquinghem	03/11/1915	05/11/1915
War Diary	Trenches I.2b. 3-5 I. 20-1	06/11/1915	06/11/1915
War Diary	Rue de Lettree.	07/11/1915	10/11/1915
War Diary	Trenches I.2b.3.5. I.20.1	11/11/1915	13/11/1915
War Diary	Rue De Biez	14/11/1915	16/11/1915
War Diary	Hallobeau.	17/11/1915	24/11/1915
War Diary	Trenches I.21.3-4 I.15.1 I.15.2 I.16	25/11/1915	28/11/1915
War Diary	Rue Marle	29/11/1915	30/11/1915
Heading	23rd Div 13th D.L.I. Vol : 5		
War Diary	Rue Marle Sheet 36 H.6.D.7.9	01/12/1915	02/12/1915
War Diary	Trenches b2.66 I.21.3-4 I 15 1-2 & I.16	03/12/1915	06/12/1915
War Diary	Armentieres (Rue Marle)	07/12/1915	10/12/1915
War Diary	Trenches b2-66 I.21.3-4 I.151-2 I.16. Sheet 30	11/12/1915	12/12/1915
War Diary	Trenches 62-66 I.21.3 And 4-I. 15.1.-2 I.16	13/12/1915	14/12/1915
War Diary	Fort Rompu H.8.c.1 1/2. 6 Sheet 36	15/12/1915	22/12/1915

War Diary	Rue Delettree (H.17 II.1/2.1/2)	23/12/1915	26/12/1915
War Diary	Trenches I.31.1-2-3-4-5 (Sheet 36)	27/12/1915	30/12/1915
War Diary	La Rolanderie (H.11.C.5.5)	31/12/1915	31/12/1915
Heading	23rd 13th D.L.I. Vol : 6 Jan.		
War Diary	La Rolanderie H.11.C.5.5	01/01/1916	03/01/1916
War Diary	Trenches I.31. 1-5 Sheet 36 N.W.4	04/01/1916	07/01/1916
War Diary	Hallobeau (H.1.B, Sheet 36)	08/01/1916	15/01/1916
War Diary	Rue Marle H.6.D.7.9 (Sheet 36 N.W.4.)	16/01/1916	19/01/1916
War Diary	Trenches I.21. 3-4 I 15.1-2 I.16	20/01/1916	23/01/1916
War Diary	Rue Marle H.6 D 6.5 Sheet 36 N.W.4	24/01/1916	27/01/1916
War Diary	Trenches I.21 (3-4) I.15 (1-2) I.1.16 Sheet 36 N.W. 4	28/01/1916	29/01/1916
War Diary	Trenches I.21. (3-4) I.15 1and 2 I.16	30/01/1916	31/01/1916
War Diary	Fort Rompu	01/02/1916	08/02/1916
War Diary	Rue de Lettree	09/02/1916	12/02/1916
War Diary	Trenches I.31. 1-5	13/02/1916	17/02/1916
War Diary	La Rolanderie H.11.C.6.5 Sheet 36	18/02/1916	21/02/1916
War Diary	Hallobeau Sheet 36 B & F.B 25.C.8.3	22/02/1916	25/02/1916
War Diary	Rue Quesnoy	26/02/1916	26/02/1916
War Diary	Morbecque Sheet 36 A D.9.C.1.7	27/02/1916	29/02/1916
Heading	23 13 D.L.I. Vol 8		
War Diary	Auchel Sheet France 36 B 3rd Ed	01/03/1916	08/03/1916
War Diary	Hermin P.22 D Sheet 36B 3rd Edition	09/03/1916	16/03/1916
War Diary	Coupigny Q.11.C.3.8 Sheet 36 B.S.E 6th Edition	17/03/1916	17/03/1916
War Diary	Calonne M.15.A.2.3	18/03/1916	21/03/1916
War Diary	Calonne Square	22/03/1916	25/03/1916
War Diary	Calonne M.15.a.2.3	25/03/1916	29/03/1916
War Diary	Bully Grenay	30/03/1916	02/04/1916
War Diary	Calonne M.15.a.2.3	02/04/1916	04/04/1916
War Diary	Calonne Trenches M.15.A.2.3	05/04/1916	06/04/1916
War Diary	Calonne M.14.B.1/2.2	07/04/1916	11/04/1916
War Diary	Calonne Trench M.15.A.2.3	12/04/1916	15/04/1916
War Diary	Bully Grenay R.11.A.3.3 Sheet 36 BSE 2	16/04/1916	18/04/1916
War Diary	Coupigny (Q.11.C.4.6)	19/04/1916	26/04/1916
War Diary	Pernes.	27/04/1916	05/05/1916
War Diary	Reclinghem	06/05/1916	19/05/1916
War Diary	Coupigny	20/05/1916	20/05/1916
War Diary	Souchez M.32.C.	21/05/1916	26/05/1916
War Diary	Bois de Noulette R.27.b.5.5	26/05/1916	30/05/1916
War Diary	Souchez M.32.C.	30/05/1916	31/05/1916
War Diary	Souchez 2 M.32 C.	01/06/1916	04/06/1916
War Diary	Ablain-St-Nazaire	05/06/1916	08/06/1916
War Diary	Coupigny Q.11.C.3.8 Sheet 36 B.S.E 6th Edition	09/06/1916	13/06/1916
War Diary	Lisbourg	14/06/1916	15/06/1916
War Diary	Delette	16/06/1916	24/06/1916
War Diary	Picquigny	25/06/1916	30/06/1916
Heading	68th Bde. 23rd Div. War Diary Brigade Temporarily Under Orders of 34th Division 16th to 20th July. 13th Battalion. Durham Light Infantry. July 1916		
War Diary	Allonville	01/07/1916	03/07/1916
War Diary	E.Q (Sheet 62 II) Albert	04/07/1916	11/07/1916
War Diary	Albert	12/07/1916	16/07/1916
War Diary	Near Pozieres	17/07/1916	20/07/1916
War Diary	Franvillers	21/07/1916	26/07/1916
War Diary	Contalmaison	27/07/1916	27/07/1916
War Diary	Near Pozieres H.Q. at X.11.B.9.7	28/07/1916	28/07/1916
War Diary	Albert	29/07/1916	31/07/1916

Heading	68th Brigade. 23rd Division. 1/13th Battalion Durham Light Infantry August 1916		
War Diary	Albert	01/08/1916	01/08/1916
War Diary	Near Contalmaison	02/08/1916	05/08/1916
War Diary	Albert	06/08/1916	07/08/1916
War Diary	La Houssoye	08/08/1916	10/08/1916
War Diary	Villers-Sous-Ailly	11/08/1916	12/08/1916
War Diary	Caistre	13/08/1916	14/08/1916
War Diary	Steenwerck	15/08/1916	15/08/1916
War Diary	Armentieres	16/08/1916	02/09/1916
War Diary	Bailleul	03/09/1916	03/09/1916
War Diary	Fletre	04/09/1916	04/09/1916
War Diary	Norbecourt	05/09/1916	11/09/1916
War Diary	Millencourt	12/09/1916	15/09/1916
War Diary	Becourt Wood	16/09/1916	16/09/1916
War Diary	Bazentin-Le-Grand	17/09/1916	19/09/1916
War Diary	Becourt Wood	20/09/1916	22/09/1916
War Diary	Support Trenches X.12 A.2.6	23/09/1916	27/09/1916
War Diary	Becourt Wood	28/09/1916	03/10/1916
War Diary	Martinpuich Trenches M.33.D.4.6	04/10/1916	06/10/1916
War Diary	Lesars Trenches M.21.D.9.7	07/10/1916	09/10/1916
War Diary	Becourt Wood	10/10/1916	11/10/1916
War Diary	Villers-Sur-Ailly	12/10/1916	13/10/1916
War Diary	St. Ricquier	14/10/1916	15/10/1916
War Diary	Winnepeg Camp H.19.A.2.5	16/10/1916	18/10/1916
War Diary	Ypres	19/10/1916	20/10/1916
War Diary	Trenches I.18 C 4 1/2. 6 Culvert	21/10/1916	23/10/1916
War Diary	Poperinghe	24/10/1916	29/10/1916
War Diary	Hospice Ypres	30/10/1916	02/11/1916
War Diary	Trenches I.21.1 to I.24.4	03/11/1916	06/11/1916
War Diary	Zillebeke Bund	07/11/1916	10/11/1916
War Diary	Winnipeg Camp	11/11/1916	16/11/1916
War Diary	Trenches I.18.4 to I.17.4	17/11/1916	20/11/1916
War Diary	Barracks Ypres	21/11/1916	24/11/1916
War Diary	Trenches I.18.4-I.17.4	25/11/1916	29/11/1916
War Diary	Winnipeg Camp	30/11/1916	07/12/1916
War Diary	The Bond	08/12/1916	16/12/1916
War Diary	Hospice Ypres	17/12/1916	23/12/1916
War Diary	Winnipeg Camp	24/12/1916	31/12/1916
War Diary	The Barracks Ypres	01/01/1917	16/01/1917
War Diary	Winnipeg Camp	17/01/1917	17/02/1917
War Diary	The Barracks Ypres.	18/02/1917	01/03/1917
War Diary	Bollezeele	02/03/1917	19/03/1917
War Diary	Houtkerque	20/03/1917	20/03/1917
War Diary	'L' Camp.	21/03/1917	21/03/1917
War Diary	'E' Camp	22/03/1917	05/04/1917
War Diary	Millam	06/04/1917	19/04/1917
War Diary	Ypres	20/04/1917	30/04/1917
War Diary	Godewaersvelde	01/05/1917	09/05/1917
War Diary	Scottish Lines	10/05/1917	19/05/1917
War Diary	Halifax Camp	20/05/1917	28/05/1917
War Diary	St Mc Adam Cappell Camp	29/05/1917	31/05/1917
War Diary	St. Macadam Cappell	01/06/1917	05/06/1917
War Diary	O Camp	06/06/1917	13/06/1917
War Diary	Mont-Des-Cats	14/06/1917	30/06/1917

Heading	13th (S) Battalion Durham Light Infantry War Diary July 1917 Volume 7. Vol 24		
Miscellaneous	From O/C 13th (S) Battn. Durham L.I.	01/08/1917	01/08/1917
War Diary	Micmac Camp	01/07/1917	18/07/1917
War Diary	Sheet 28 N.W. H.21d.9.1	19/07/1917	21/07/1917
War Diary	Mont Des Cats	22/07/1917	30/07/1917
War Diary	Wizernes	31/07/1917	09/08/1917
War Diary	Moulle	10/08/1917	24/08/1917
War Diary	Palace Camp	25/08/1917	29/08/1917
War Diary	Dickebusch	30/08/1917	31/08/1917
Heading	War Diary of 13th. (S) Battalion, The Durham Light Infantry. From. 1st Sept. 1917. To. 30th Sept. 1917. Vol 26		
War Diary	Dickebusch	01/09/1917	03/09/1917
War Diary	Steenvoorde	04/09/1917	05/09/1917
War Diary	Noordpeene	06/09/1917	13/09/1917
War Diary	Steenvoorde	14/09/1917	14/09/1917
War Diary	Chippawa Camp	15/09/1917	16/09/1917
War Diary	Dickebusch	17/09/1917	24/09/1917
War Diary	York Camp Westoutre	25/09/1917	28/09/1917
War Diary	Ascot Camp Westoutre	29/09/1917	01/10/1917
War Diary	Berthen Area	02/10/1917	02/10/1917
War Diary	Mont Des Cats	03/10/1917	08/10/1917
War Diary	Ascot Camp Westoutre	09/10/1917	09/10/1917
War Diary	Scottish Wood	10/10/1917	13/10/1917
War Diary	Bund	14/10/1917	14/10/1917
War Diary	N.2.b.2.7	15/10/1917	17/10/1917
War Diary	Railway Dugouts	18/10/1917	22/10/1917
War Diary	Tatinghem	23/10/1917	31/10/1917

WO95/2187/2

13 Bn Durham Light Inf.

Sep 1914 – Oct 1917

23RD DIVISION
68TH INFY BDE

13TH BN DURHAM LT INFY
AUG 1914 - AUG 1917 OCT

TO ITALY

23 DIV
68 BDE

BEF

13th Battn.
  Durham Light Infantry.

August 1914 — August 1915

Went to Western Front
 as 12 Battalion in Aug 15 —
69 Inf Bde
23 Div.

121/6607

23rd Division

13th D.L.I.

Vol: I

From 24 - 31. 8. 15
Aug '18

WAR DIARY or INTELLIGENCE SUMMARY

Army Form C. 2118

(Erase heading not required.)

Place	Date	Hour	Summary of Events and Information	Remarks and references to Appendices
BULLSWATER	17.9.14		Battalion formed out of a draft of recruits enlisted at Newcastle and vicinity MAJOR N.T. BIDDULPH Commanding, Lt C.E. WALKER Adjutant.	
	22.9.14		COL G.A. ASHBY C.B. assumed command	
	30.9.14		Battalion moved to ALDERSHOT (Malplaquet Barracks)	
	24.1.14		Battalion moved into billets at WOKINGHAM	
	9.2.15		Battalion moved to ALDERSHOT (Malplaquet Barracks)	
	28.2.15		Battalion moved by rail to ASHFORD, KENT. (billets)	
HINDHEAD	23.5.15 11.30am		Battalion moved by rail to BRAMSHOTT, HANTS (billets) Inspected by H.M. THE KING	
BRAMSHOTT	8.7.15		COL G.A. ASHBY C.B. relinquished the command of the Battalion, Lt. Col. J.R. O'CONNELL appointed to command.	
BRAMSHOTT	23.8.15		MAJOR N.T. BIDDULPH appointed to command Battalion vice Lt. Col. J.R. O'CONNELL resigned	

N.T. Biddulph
COMMANDING 13th Bn. DURHAM LIGHT INFY

Army Form C. 2118

One sheet only

WAR DIARY or INTELLIGENCE SUMMARY

(Erase heading not required.)

Instructions regarding War Diaries and Intelligence Summaries are contained in F. S. Regs, Part II. and the Staff Manual respectively. Title Pages will be prepared in manuscript.

Place	Date	Hour	Summary of Events and Information	Remarks and references to Appendices
GULLSWATER	7.9.14		Battalion formed out of a draft of recruits enlisted at Newcastle and vicinity. MAJOR N.T. BIDDULPH Commanding, LT C.E. WALKER adjutant.	
	22.9.14		COL G.A. ASHBY C.B. assumed command.	
	30.9.14		Battalion moved to ALDERSHOT (Malplaquet Barracks)	
	24.1.14		Battalion moved into billets at WOKINGHAM	
	9.2.15		Battalion moved to ALDERSHOT (Malplaquet Barracks)	
	28.2.15		Battalion moved by rail to ASHFORD, KENT. (billets)	
	23.5.15		Battalion moved by rail to BRAMSHOTT, HANTS. (billets)	
HINDHEAD	20.5.15 11.30am		Battalion inspected by H.M. THE KING	
BRAMSHOTT	8.7.15		COL G.A. ASHBY C.B. relinquished the command of the Battalion, Lt.Col. J.R. O'CONNELL appointed to command.	
BRAMSHOTT	23.8.15		MAJOR N.T. BIDDULPH appointed to command Battalion vice Lt.Col. J. R. O'CONNELL resigned	

EB

Christopher [?]
Lt.Col.
COMMANDING 13th Bn DURHAM LIGHT INFY.

Army Form C. 2118

WAR DIARY
or
INTELLIGENCE SUMMARY
(Erase heading not required.)

Instructions regarding War Diaries and Intelligence Summaries are contained in F. S. Regs., Part II. and the Staff Manual respectively. Title Pages will be prepared in manuscript.

Place	Date	Hour	Summary of Events and Information	Remarks and references to Appendices
BRAMSHOTT CAMP	25 Aug 15	9.40 am	Transport and Machine Gun Sections entrained at Liphook and proceeded overseas via Southampton and HAVRE	
	25.8.15	7.55 pm 8.25 pm	A. & B. Coys entrained at Liphook, and proceeded to FOLKESTONE; embarked on { transport 2031; landed at BOULOGNE and C. & D. " " " " " { transport " " " " " " " marched to BOULOGNE Rest Camp, arriving there 4 am 26.8.15	
	27.8.15		Battalion entrained at PONT-DE-BRIQUES, joining transport which had arrived from HAVRE, and moved to WATTEN, arriving 8 a.m; detrained and marched to MOULLE — 7 km; went into billets at MOULLE. Strength Officers 31 (including M.O. and Chaplain) other ranks 936 (excluding attached; Orderly Room Sgt. at Base and 2 men in Hospital at BOULOGNE	
MOULLE	31.8.15		2/Lt. G.H. BAILEY went into hospital	

W.T. Biddulph
COMMANDING 13th Bn DURHAM LIGHT INFY

68/27

13th Jan'y.
Vol: 2

121/7761

23rd Novemr

Sep 1. 15

Army Form C. 2118.

WAR DIARY 13th DURHAM L.I.
INTELLIGENCE SUMMARY

Vol. ii. September '15

(Erase heading not required.)

Instructions regarding War Diaries and Intelligence Summaries are contained in F. S. Regs., Part II. and the Staff Manual respectively. Title pages will be prepared in manuscript.

Place	Date	Hour	Summary of Events and Information	Remarks and references to Appendices
MOVLLE	1.9.15		Training. Weather fine.	
"	2.9.15		Weather fine — Training	
"	3.9.15		" " — Training	
"	4.9.15		" " — Training	
"	5.9.15		" " — Training	
"	6.9.15	5.58 a.m.	68th Infantry Bde left MOVLLE (13th D.L.I. 5.53 a.m.) and marched to HAZEBROUCK via TILQUES, ST MARTIN and ARQUES; distance about 16 miles. Weather hot. 3 Companies billeted in HAZEBROUCK, one Coy bivouacked.	
HAZEBROUCK	7.9.15	9.28 a.m.	68th Inf Bde left HAZEBROUCK and proceeded to STEENWERCK via BORRE, STRA=ZEELE; billeted in STEENWERCK. Weather hot. 37 N.C.O.s and men left in C.C.S. HAZEBROUCK.	
STEENWERCK	8.9.15	4.2 p.m.	12th & 13th D.L.I. inspected by Lieut. Gen. Sir. W.P. Pulteney K.C.B., D.S.O. commanding 3rd Corps	
"	9.9.15	5.55 p.m.	13th D.L.I. left STEENWERCK by Companies at 15 min intervals, arrived SAILLY BRIDGE (Sheet 36 G.16, C.7.6) 7p.m. to 7.45 p.m.: 2 Platoons each Coy attached as follows; A. Co to 11. C. L.I.: B & C coys to 13th KINGS LIVERPOOLS: remaining Platoons attached SOMERSET L.I. in billets RUE DE QUESNE. Casualties 1 O.R. wounded	
SAILLY on LYS	10.9.15		Remaining two platoons proceeded to trenches & Battalions their companies were attached to, relieving Platoons which entered trenches the previous night, whilst evacuating trenches of D.C.L.I. 2 Platoons of A Coy under	

WAR DIARY
or
INTELLIGENCE SUMMARY.
(Erase heading not required.)

Army Form C. 2118.

Place	Date	Hour	Summary of Events and Information	Remarks and references to Appendices
SAILLY-SUR-LYS	11.9.15		Capt U.S. NAYLOR and Lt BUTTERWORTH at about 7.15 p.m. were caught by M.G. fire, Casualties O.R. 5 of which 1 slightly – at duty. Saw German Taube brought down by H.A. fire. Weather fine. 68th Inf. Bde attached 20th Div. (Auth. Telegram 61st Inf/Bde) 1st M.G. Section under Lieut. MARKHAM went into 12th KINGS LIVERPOOL trench 3.30 p.m. – No casualties – Weather fine.	
"	12.9.15		Operations quiet. – Weather fine. 1st M.G. Section under Lt. H.R. MARKHAM remained in 12th KINGS LIVERPOOL trench another day, whilst SOMERSET L.I. relieved 12th KINGS LIVERPOOLS. German 5" gun shelled old gun emplacement and farmhouse H.33.c.10.5 250 yds. E. of Battalion H.Q. – One O.R. K.O.Y.L.I. Killed. No casualties K.L.I.	
"	13.9.15	12/th 7.20 p.m. 12/th	1st M.G. Section under Lt H.R MARKHAM evacuated their trench leaving behind 3 N.C.O.s and 7 men; 2nd M.G. Section under Lt G.M. LONG relieving 1st Section 3.20 p.m. At 4.25 a.m. a mine exploded in the trench occupied by a M.G. Section SOMERSET L.I. burying the gun and killing and wounding all the gun crew. The explosion was immediately followed by a H.E. Shrapnel bombardment directed at the same place. About 10 minutes later our batteries opened fire at parapet directly opposite the mine, blowing parapet to pieces. No casualties 2L.I. M.G. Section. At about 12.30 a.m. 13.9.15 whilst evacuating trench occupied by	

WAR DIARY
or
INTELLIGENCE SUMMARY.
(Erase heading not required.)

Army Form C. 2118.

Place	Date	Hour	Summary of Events and Information	Remarks and references to Appendices
			Somerset L.I. stray bullets struck 2 O.R. (wounded) at 3:10 pm. 13.9.15 German batteries opened with shrapnel on Battn H.Q. (H.33.d.4.b) one shell exploding on roof of Orderly Room. Weather fine.	
SAILLYSURAYS	14.9.15		Rained slightly a.m. Lt. Long with 2nd M.G. to remain in trenches to 15.9.15. B.Cº and 2 Platoons D.Cº proceeded to ESTAIRES (a.25.c.9.6) under Major C.E. WALKER - At 5:35 pm. German battery fired several rounds shrapnel at British aeroplane flying E of and above Battn H.Q. 3 rounds striking Orderly Room.	
SAILLY-SURAYS	15.9.15		Weather cloudy; rain during night. 2 Platoon D Cº who returned from trenches at 11:30 p.m. 14.9.15 proceeded under Capt. A.H. FAUSTIN at 8:30 a.m. to join detachment in billets at ESTAIRES.— 2nd M.G. Section under Lt. G.M. LONG returned from Somerset L.I. trenches 5:30 pm. No casualties.	
"	16.9.15		Weather fine.	
"	17.9.15		Battalion moved from billets in SAILLY and ESTAIRES meeting at crossroads (SAILLY) at 3:10 a.m. and proceeded to bivouacs at PETIT MOULIN arriving 5 a.m.	
PETIT-MOULIN	18.9.15		Weather fine. Battalion furnished two working parties, one of 400, one of 200 men for reserve trenches. A.Cº 1st party shelled 4:20 p.m. whilst working and returned 7:30 p.m. 2nd party returned 12:15 a.m. 19.9.15.	

Army Form C. 2118.

WAR DIARY
or
INTELLIGENCE SUMMARY.
(Erase heading not required.)

Instructions regarding War Diaries and Intelligence Summaries are contained in F. S. Regs., Part II. and the Staff Manual respectively. Title pages will be prepared in manuscript.

Place	Date	Hour	Summary of Events and Information	Remarks and references to Appendices
PETIT-MOULIN dépôt	20.9.15		Sunday. Weather fine.	
"	21.9.15		Weather fine, cold. Wind East.	
"			Weather fine, cold. N.E. Wind. - Working parties as follows:- A Co. 1 Off. 50 O.R. at I.G.C.3.4. at 9 pm; returned 2.30 a.m./ 22.9.15 ; C. Co. 1 Off. 50 O.R. at I.G.C.3.4. at 10.30 pm; returned 4.30 a.m. 22.9.15: no casualties	
"	22.9.15		Weather fine; full moon.	
"	23.9.15		Weather cloudy; rained all night 23/24. Working parties: 1 Capt, 2 Subs, 200 O.R. at LA VESLE Post; 1 Capt. 2 Subs, 150 O.R. at La FLEURIS POST both 6.30pm. No casualties. Severe bombardment all day on German lines.	
"	24.9.15		Rain; severe bombardment all day and during nights 23/24 and 24/25. At 5 pm a German battery opened on an English Aeroplane flying over our lines and wounded 6 O.R.	
"	25.9.15		Cloudy at first, then heavy rain. Wind S.W. to N.	
		1. am	Received following message from G.H.Q.:- "I am wished to inform troops to be informed that he feels confident they will realize how much our success in the forthcoming operations depends upon the individual efforts of each Officer, N.C.O. and man and he wishes this to be conveyed to them, in such a manner as not to disclose our intentions to the enemy."	
		4.33 am	Battalion roused and fed.	
		5.10 am	Received message from 66th Bde H.Q. as follows:- "3rd Corps report) MEERUT Division got in pretty easily over enemy	

Army Form C. 2118.

WAR DIARY
or
INTELLIGENCE SUMMARY.
(Erase heading not required.)

Place	Date	Hour	Summary of Events and Information	Remarks and references to Appendices
PETIT-MOULIN	26.9.15		"reported to be surrendering fairly freely ... two Battalions 8th Division reported in German 3rd line trenches" Weather wet: wind W.S.W	
		11.23am	Received wire from 68th Inf. Bde. stating that Brigade was attached to 20th Division and would move at 3pm.	
		1.53pm	Received wire from 68th Inf Bde ordering billeting parties proceed to ESTAIRES	
		3.30pm	Battalion left PETIT MOULIN arriving ESTAIRES about 5.30pm. Completed billeting arrangements in RUE BASSEE 11pm. Ascertained from G.O.C. 68th Inf Bde that Bde was in support of MEERUT Division which had been driven back into its own trenches with heavy casualties.	
ESTAIRES	27.9.15		Cloudy slight rain.	
		10.30am	Received message (B.M.O. 80 d/27.9.15) that the 68th Inf Bde would return to its former billets at PETIT MOULIN; both DURHAM battalions being under the command of Lt.Col. ELWES 12th D.L.I.	
		2.30pm	Left ESTAIRES arrived PETIT MOULIN 4.50pm. Received 1st Draft; 9 N.C.O.s and men from 17th (Serv) Batt. DURHAM L.I. at STEENWERCKS. 2/Lt F.A.BROWN sent to conduct them to unit.	
PETIT-MOULIN	28.9.15		Battalion moved 2.30pm from PETIT-MOULIN to ESTAIRES via CROIX-DU-BAC; billets C & D Coys near Bridge over river; A & B Coys and transport in RUE DU-BOIS. Battalion attached 20th Division.— Weather wet.	
ESTAIRES	29.9.15		Weather wet and cold. One packhorse shot by Sgt. A.V.C. having been	

Army Form C. 2118.

WAR DIARY
or
INTELLIGENCE SUMMARY.

(Erase heading not required.)

Instructions regarding War Diaries and Intelligence Summaries are contained in F. S. Regs., Part II. and the Staff Manual respectively. Title pages will be prepared in manuscript.

Place	Date	Hour	Summary of Events and Information	Remarks and references to Appendices
ESTAIRES	32.9.15		kicked during the night and breaking a leg. Weather wet and cold. A. & H. Coy provided tunnelling party (to report to H.Q. 173 mining Co.) 2 officers 8 N.C.O.s and 75 men.	

W J Beckwith Lt Col.
COMMANDING 13th Bn DURHAM LIGHT INFY

23/10 Bowden

20 Oct attached 24 h trade
till Nov 2nd only

13th Sept.
Vol 3

Oct 15

12/
7/4 30

Army Form C. 2118

WAR DIARY
or
INTELLIGENCE SUMMARY
(Erase heading not required.)

Instructions regarding War Diaries and Intelligence Summaries are contained in F.S. Regs., Part II. and the Staff Manual respectively. Title Pages will be prepared in manuscript.

Place	Date	Hour	Summary of Events and Information	Remarks and references to Appendices
ESTAIRES	1.10.15		Weather warm, fine.	
	2.10.15		" " "	
	3.10.15		" " "	
	4.10.15		" wet; Battalion moved 9 a.m. from billets in ESTAIRES to PETIT MOULIN; arrived PETIT MOULIN 11.15 a.m. — Battalion moved from PETIT MOULIN 5.30 p.m; arrived in billets S. of ERQUINGHEM in RUE DE BIEZ and RUE DE LETTRES 6.30 p.m.	
	5.10.15		Weather wet	
	6.10.15		Weather cloudy. Wind 7.30 a.m. N.W. — Whilst on working party at TRAMWAY FARM I.19.B.0.4. No 16768 Pte F. Pilcher B Co wounded by stray bullet.	
Trenches 55-58	7.10.15		Weather dull — Battalion moved from billets at ERQUINGHEM and took over Trenches 55-58 from 12th Durham Light Infantry; relief finished 10.10 p.m. Officers patrol under Lt. Tait went out in front of our line at 1.30 a.m. — Reinforcement arrived STEENWERCK (52 men) and proceeded to transport lines at L'EPINETTE.	
"	8.10.15		Weather dull.— Wind 9.40 a.m.— light, northerly. Enemy quiet, except snipers in front of A Co. French 55 (I.26.3).—Casualties:— No 23650 Pte J.W. BRETT B Co. died of wounds 8.10.15 17667 Sgt. J.T. JOHNSON A Co. wounded. 19014 Pte W. BAXTER B Co. accidental.	
"	9.10.15		Weather cloudy; enemy parapet visible 6 a.m. — Wind 7.30 a.m., light	

WAR DIARY
or
INTELLIGENCE SUMMARY
(Erase heading not required.)

Army Form C. 2118

Place	Date	Hour	Summary of Events and Information	Remarks and references to Appendices
Trenches 55-58	10.10.15		N.E. Enemy quiet except for snipers; a few shells fell near BURNT FARM at about 4 p.m. Casualty :- No 16300 Pte G. BROWN A Co killed rifle grenade. Weather finer. - Wind: 9.10 a.m. light, south east; 7.55 p.m. northeasterly. Casualty :- 23647 Pte E. BRASS A. Co, severely wounded, died 6.45 a.m. 11.10.15 Enemy put air 4.2 shells over right half of TRENCH 56 (I 20.1), two bursting short of parapet.	
	11.10.15		Weather cloudy at first, fine later. - Wind 8.30 a.m. - light, easterly. Enemy bombarded the front line of the division from 10.- a.m. to 11.15 with H.E. Shrapnel and some long bangs; about 200 shells fell in II Coys area (I.20.1), only two striking parapet, and breaking it slightly. At about 11.30 a.m. to 12 noon enemy put 8 shrapnel (percussion) and Strike fire) into Ration Farm and at 4.50 p.m. six shells. - No casualties 13th D.L.I. - German aeroplane after duel with British aeroplane brought down and fell at H.17.B.3.8. at 4.35 p.m.	
12.10.15 ERQUINGHEM (South)	12.10.15		Weather fine. - Battalion relieved by 12th DURHAM L.I. 8.30 a.m. and moved into "C" Battalion area BOIS GRENIER; A and D Coys in billets RUE DIE LETTREE. Casualties :- No 23439 Pte R. GOTT A Co killed 3 a.m. 24513 " J. WORTON B Co wounded; accidental 24607 " D. NELSON B Co wounded; accidental	
	13.10.15		Weather wet. Wind 8.30 a.m. S.W. - Received draft 52 men from transport	

WAR DIARY or INTELLIGENCE SUMMARY

Army Form C. 2118

(Erase heading not required.)

Place	Date	Hour	Summary of Events and Information	Remarks and references to Appendices
BOIS GRENIER	14.10.15		Officer. Some sniping near Battalion Hdqts dugout. Casualty: No 24751 Pte T. Moody B Co wounded (by shrapnel exploding 300 yds away). Weather dull. Wind - S.am. S.S.E.	
	15.10.15		Weather dull, cold. - Wind 8.am. S.E.	
Trenches 55-58	16.10.15		Weather damp, cloudy. Battalion left BOIS GRENIER line and took over trenches 55-58 (I.26.3 - I.26.4 - I.26.5 - I.26.1) from 12th Durham L.I. 8 p.m. No casualties.	
	17.10.15		Weather dull and cold. Wind - 9 a.m. - light N.E. - At 3.35 p.m. a sniper was reported in a tree at I.20.D.8.5. 2 bombs from our catapult were fired at him, and the machine gun from H coys trench (No 58. I.20.1) enfiladed the enemys parapet. --- A sniper patrol consisting of No 18792 L.Cpl. W. CLAIRE H Co and No 19644 Pte R. HICKSON DCo went out from A Co (I.26.3) at 4.30 am, with orders to return at 7.30 am; at dawn on the 17th they shot two Germans who showed themselves above the parapet but were thereafter so watched that they could not return. Snipers until 8.30 am. on the 18.10.15; they reported no German snipers left the trench whilst they were there.	
	18.10.15		Weather fine am; cloudy pm. Enemy fired 3 shells just beyond support I.20.1. Between 10.20 am and 11.20 am. enemy fired 29 rounds shrapnel at PARK ROW near Ration Farm. - A small offensive patrol under direction of Capt: V.S. Naylor left Trench I.26.3. at 7.30 p.m. with the object of driving out working party in ditch discovered by L-Cpl. CLAIRE on 18.10.15. 2/Lt. SAUERBECK proceeded	

Army Form C. 2118

WAR DIARY
or
INTELLIGENCE SUMMARY
(Erase heading not required.)

Place	Date	Hour	Summary of Events and Information	Remarks and references to Appendices
JESUS FARM.	20.10.15		advance and threw 2 bombs in the trench. Whereupon our M.G. opened fire and swept the enemy parapet and C/103 battery opened fired with section salvoes H.E. on the enemy parapet. Whilst returning to the trench 2/Lt. SAUERBECK was struck by a bomb. Casualties:— 2/Lt. G.H. BAILEY dangerously wounded in the head while using a battery on some high ground in rear of T.I.26.4. (dying 6.a.m. 20.10.15) 2/Lt. C.T.W. SAUERBECK wounded. No. 23924 Pte J. PEARSON C. Cº accidently " 17115 " H. STRINGER C. Cº killed " 20505 " G. STRONG A. Cº " 18721 " R. GASKELL D. Cº slightly " 23924 " J. PEARSON Cº accidently	
	21.10.15		Weather warm - damp. - The Battalion moved into billets at JESUS FARM handing over trenches I.26.3., I.26.4., I.26.5 and I.20.1. at 12th D.L.I. at 8.15 p.m.: attached 24th Inf. Bde.	
	22.10.15		Weather warm. - Funeral of 2/Lt. G.H. BAILEY at BAILLEUL. 10 a.m. Weather colder. - Whilst on working party at Fme DESPLANQUES (I.14.D) under Capt. BLAKE at 6 p.m. No. 24798 Sgt./R. HENDERSON DCº wounded. Reinforcement received 2 N.C.Os and 20 men.	
	23.10.15		Weather misty.	
	24.10.15		Weather cold. - Wind E.N.E.	
	25.10.15		Weather wet, raining all day; cold wind E.N.E.	
	26.10.15		" " " nearly " " ; wind southwest.	

Army Form C. 2118.

WAR DIARY
or
~~INTELLIGENCE SUMMARY~~

(Erase heading not required.)

Place	Date	Hour	Summary of Events and Information	Remarks and references to Appendices
JESUS FARM	27.10.15		Weather showery; wind south	
	28.10.15		" wet ~~cloudy~~ ; wind south #	
	29.10.15		" Cloudy " "	
	30.10.15		" " " "	
	31.10.15		" fine; wind 9 a.m. Easterly	

W.T. Biddulph Lt.Col.
COMMANDING 13th Bn DURHAM LIGHT INFY

13th Oct 29.
fol: 4

121/7624

23rd Hussein

Nov 15.

13th D.L.I.

WAR DIARY or INTELLIGENCE SUMMARY

Army Form C. 2118.

Place	Date	Hour	Summary of Events and Information	Remarks and references to Appendices
JESUS FARM	1.11.15		Weather wet	
"	2.11.15		Weather wet. Battalion left JESUS FARM 4.30 p.m. and took trenches I.26.3.5 and I.20.1 at 8.25 p.m. from 12th DURHAM L.I. Enemy very quiet rain all night. Casualties: O.R. one wounded.	
Trenches near ERQUINGHEM	3.11.15		Wind fresh north. Weather wet. Trenches inundated, parapets and dugouts caving in. Enemy quiet.	
"	4.11.15		Weather wet. Wind Northerly. Very misty. Lieut. P.A. BROWN whilst superintending working party on the wire, went towards the German parapet opposite I.26.4 at 9.15 p.m. accompanied by No. 17424 Pte. T. KENNY: after being his direction in the fog they found themselves near the German parapet. Lieut. BROWN was shot through both thighs. Pte KENNY, although the enemy fire was heavy tried to carry the officer back to our lines and when the fog became better crawled through. Being nearly exhausted he made the officer as comfortable as he could and came to our lines for help; and succeeded in guiding a party of officers back to where the officer lay. A hostile party had however crept up in the meantime and attacked the rescue party on its way back to our trenches. Capt. G. WHITE thereupon sent the party on with the wounded officer and stood the enemy off with a rifle. CASUALTIES: Lt. P.A. BROWN killed; O.R. two killed, one wounded.	
"	5.11.15		Misty. Wind S.E. — Enemy shelled trench I.26.3 about 11. a.m. no damage our artillery — 18 pounder replied with salvoes, the first 3 shells bursted over main	

Army Form C. 2118.

WAR DIARY
or
INTELLIGENCE SUMMARY.
(Erase heading not required.)

Instructions regarding War Diaries and Intelligence Summaries are contained in F. S. Regs., Part II. and the Staff Manual respectively. Title pages will be prepared in manuscript.

Place	Date	Hour	Summary of Events and Information	Remarks and references to Appendices
Trenches I.26.3-5 I.20.1	6.11.15		under German parapet opposite Trench I.26.4, remainder falling behind I.26.4. Casualties Nil. Wind N.W. Battalion handed over trenches I.26.3-5, I.20.1 to 12th DURHAM L.I. 7.15 p.m. occupying L Battalion billets in BOIS GRENIER LINE and RUE DE LETTREE 6.30 p.m. Casualties nil.	
Rue de Lettree	7.11.15		Weather dull cold	
	8.11.15		Weather fine. Wind S.E. light.	
	9.11.15		Weather fine in morning, rainstorm afternoon and evening. Strong wind S.W. Enemy shelled C. Battalion trenches in morning and vicinity of GRISPOT from 1.30 p.m. to 2.15 p.m. Casualty one O.R. accidentally.	
	10.11.15		Wind S.E. light. Battalion moved into trenches I.26.3-5, I.20.1 relieving 12th DURHAM L.I. who took over C. Battalion billets	
Trenches I.26.3-5 I.20.1	11.11.15		Wind S.W. rain. Enemy shelled GRISPOT, LA VESEE and BOIS GRENIER heavily from 9.45 a.m. to 12 noon. Casualties: 1 O.R. killed, two wounded.	
	12.11.15		Wind S.W. stronger; some rain. Casualties: 1 O.R. wounded accidently.	
	13.11.15		Wind S.W. stronger, rain all previous night. Battalion handed over trenches I.26.3-5 and I.20.I to 12th DURHAM L.I. and moved to D. Batt. area RUE DE BIEZ and RUE DE LETTREE. No 24622 Pte A.E. LEET killed. Chararter ?	

WAR DIARY
INTELLIGENCE SUMMARY

Army Form C. 2118.

Place	Date	Hour	Summary of Events and Information	Remarks and references to Appendices
RUE DE BIEZ	15.11.15		A German sniper opposite I.26.3. Casualties:- two O.R. one killed accidentally	
"	15.11.15		Wind slight N.W. Casualties nil.	
"	16.11.15		Wind S.W. - Casualties nil.	
"	16.11.15		Wind S.S.E. - Rain - night cold - Battalion was relieved in "D" Battalion billets by 2nd E.LANCS. Rest at 5.30 pm and moved into billets vacated by them at HALLOBEAU.	
HALLOBEAU	17.11.15		Frost during night of 16/17th - Rain during day.	
"	18.11.15		Frost during night of 17/18 - Rain during day. Cold	
"	19.11.15		Frost during night of 18/19 - Cold.	
"	20.11.15		Frost during night of 19/20 - cold	
"	21.11.15		Frost during night of 20/21 - cold.	
"	22.11.15		Frost during night of 21/22 - cold : noon cloudy.	
"	23.11.15		Frost during night of 22/23	
"	24.11.15		Weather warmer - Wind W.N.W. Battalion left billets at HALLOBEAU and took over trenches I.21.3 and 4, I.15.1 and 2 and I.16 from 8th W.YORKS (Lt Col. — STEPHENS commanding). No casualties.	
Trenches I.21.3.4 I.15.1 I.15.2 I.16	25.11.15		Wind N.W. - Weather colder. 2/Lt. R.H. Stubbs with draft of 15 O.R. and following officers joined the Battalion : Lt. N.A. TARGET, 2/Lt. J.A.H. OLIPHANT and 2/Lt. H.J.L PARKER Casualties: One O.R. wounded. Chevalier Meeper	

WAR DIARY
or
INTELLIGENCE SUMMARY.

(Erase heading not required.)

Army Form C. 2118.

Place	Date	Hour	Summary of Events and Information	Remarks and references to Appendices
Trenches F.2, 3.4.2.15.12. I.16.	26.11.15		Wind N.W. cold. Enemy quiet. No casualties.	
"	27.11.15	12.0pm	Wind N.E. night very cold. German Artillery opened on working party to right of Distillery in 3 minutes after being informed; enemy retaliated by shelling CHAPELLE d'ARMENTIERES and Battalion H.Q. Casualties nil :- 2 O.R. wounded.	
		2.pm		
		3.15am		
"	28.11.15		Wind N.E. mild. Enemy quiet but shelled CHAPELLE d'ARMENTIERES at intervals during morning. Battn handed over trenches to 12th DURHAM L.I. and proceeded to C. Battalion area RUE MARLE. Casualties nil	
		7.10pm		
RUE MARLE	29.11.15		Wind light S.E. Rain.	
"	30.11.15		Wind S.E. Rain	

Sweeney, Major
for Lt. Col.
COMMANDING 15th Bn DURHAM LIGHT INFY.

13 ہ ستمبر
vol: 5

121/7936

23 ۔۔۔

WAR DIARY
or
INTELLIGENCE SUMMARY
(Erase heading not required.)

13th DURHAM L.I.

Army Form C. 2118.

Vol. VI December 1915

Place	Date	Hour	Summary of Events and Information	Remarks and references to Appendices
RUE MARLE Sheet 36 H.6.D.7.9.	1.12.15		Wind S.S.E. – Rain.	
"	2.12.15		Wind S. to S.W. – Battalion left billets in RUE MARLE and took over trenches 62-66 I.21 3-4, I.15 1-2 and I.16 from 12th D.L.I. at 6.55 p.m Casualties:- one O.R. wounded. 10th N.F. on our right.	
Trenches 62.66 3.12.15 I.21.3-4, I.15 1-2 & I.16.	3.12.15		Wind E. light. – Rain. Enemy shelled ARMENTIERES; also saturdump; shell went through reg. Bde. signal office. Casualties:- one O.R. killed, one wounded.	
"	4.12.15		Wind S.W. strong during night of 4/5. Rain. – Battalion received reinforcement of 1 officer from 17th D.L.I. 2/Lt. T.G. SAINT. – Enemy shelled ARMENTIERES doing damage to houses and roads near RUE MARLE corner. Casualties nil.	
"	5.12.15		Wind 7.30 a.m. W. – Patrol from I.21.2 (A Coy) consisting of No 18513 Cpl. W. HORNBY and No 21603 Pte L.C. WORTON both A.Coy left at 11.30 p.m. to examine German House (I.21.B.1½.1.); they could not owing to French were having heavy preparations lately placed round it; examine the house thoroughly; they they proceeded along the German line until hearing voices behind the parapet they threw 3 over bombs, causing great uproar; and returned to our trenches 2.30 a.m. on the 5th. Enemy shelled ARMENTIERES 3.55 p.m to 4.10 p.m. Casualties: 1 O.R. two wounded, at duty.	

WAR DIARY or INTELLIGENCE SUMMARY.

(Erase heading not required.)

Army Form C. 2118.

Vol V. December 1915

Place	Date	Hour	Summary of Events and Information	Remarks and references to Appendices
Trenches 12-66 I.21.3-4, I.15.1-2 J.1.16	6.12.15		Fine in morning, rain during afternoon. Our Artillery shelled the enemy trenches from 12 noon till 3pm. Enemy replied with 20 shells. Battalion handed over trenches to 12th D.L.I. and marched into billets in N Battalion area RUE MARLE. (H.6.D.7.3) Sheet 36. Casualties:- OR one killed one wounded	
ARMENTIERES (RUE MARLE)	7.12.15		Wind S.W. – Strong.	
"	8.12.15	2 p.m.	Enemy fired 6 shells near C. & D Coy Billets – No Casualties Wind S.W. fresh.	
"	9.12.15	2 p.m.	Enemy shelled D Coys billets, no casualties. Wind S.E. Wet. –	
"	10.12.15		Enemy shelled ERQUINGHEM and ARMENTIERES – no casualties. Wind S.W. light. Some shelling in RUE MARLE by enemy during afternoon. Battalion took over trenches 62-66 (I.21.3 and 4; I.15.1 and 2; and I.16) from 12th D.L.I. at 7.15 p.m. Casualties nil. – Received reinforcement O.R. 30.	
Trenches 62-66 I.21.3.4. I.15.1.2 I.16. Sect. 36.	11.12.15		Wind S.S.E. Our artillery shelled German house and salient at I.21.B.4.B from 12 noon to 3 p.m. Enemy replied and fired 3 shells in our support trenches. Casualties O.R. 1 wounded.	
"	12.12.15		Wind N.W. Our artillery cutting wire opposite trench 64. Redistribution of Battalion; A and D Coys occupying front line; one platoon each of B, C Coy	

Army Form C. 2118.

WAR DIARY
or
INTELLIGENCE SUMMARY
(Erase heading not required.)

Vol. V. December 1915

Place	Date	Hour	Summary of Events and Information	Remarks and references to Appendices
Trenches 13.12.15 I.21.3 and 4 - I.15.1-2 I.16.	13.12.15		in support on flanks; remaining six platoons in reserve in BOIS GRENIER line. Casualties nil. Wind N.W. Artillery out wire at I.21.b.3.4½. Officers patrol from I.16. during night - no casualties	
	14.12.15	12 noon 3 pm 6.20	Wind W. Frost night of 9/11/12; day cold and clear. Our artillery fired 100 shells at Germans' House (I.21.d). Enemy replied by shelling Battalion H.Q. in the Orchard - fired about 20 shells. The Battalion was relieved at 6.20 pm by 2nd E.Lancs Regt and marched into billets at FORT ROMPU. No casualties	
FORT ROMPU H.8.C.1½.6 Sheet 36.	15.12.15		Weather cold but fine. The Battalion paraded as strong as possible at 10.15 am and proceeded to H.Q.6.2.18 where the 3rd Army Commander Lt. Gen. Sir W. Pulteney K.C.B., D.S.O., in the presence of representatives from all Units in the Corps presented the ribbon of the Victoria Cross to No 17424 L.Sgt. T. KENNY "B" Company, 13th D.L.I. for an act of gallantry on the night of Nov. 4.1915. Wind W. - Rain -	
"	16.12.15		Wind S.E. - Rain night of 15/16 and on 16th.	
"	17.12.15		At 9.30 am, Major Gen. J.M. Babbington C.B., C.M.G. G.O.C. 23rd Division presented the ribbon of the D.C.M. to No 21603 Pte J.C. WORTON, A Co. 13th D.L.I.; at conclusion finished carried out in the field. General Babbington subsequently visited	

Army Form C. 2118.

WAR DIARY
or
INTELLIGENCE SUMMARY.
(Erase heading not required.)

Vol. V. Dec. 1915

Instructions regarding War Diaries and Intelligence Summaries are contained in F. S. Regs., Part II. and the Staff Manual respectively. Title pages will be prepared in manuscript.

Place	Date	Hour	Summary of Events and Information	Remarks and references to Appendices
FORT ROMPU H.S.C.1½.6 Sheet 36	16.12.15		the both Field Ambulance and made a similar presentation to No 18513 Cpl. W. HORNBY A Co. Wind S.E. some rain. No casualties	
"	19.12.15		Wind N-N.E. rain. Reinforcement: 2/Lt. S.R.D. TYSSEN formerly with 12th D.L.I. joined the Battalion from 16th D.L.I. - no casualties	
"	20.12.15		Wind N.E. Rain - Zeppelin reported over POPPERINGHE & PONT BALLOT at 8.45 pm and 10.30 pm by 51st & 64th Inf Bdes and 21st Div.	
"	21.12.15		Wind N.W. Showers	
"	22.12.15		Wind S.W. 10 m.p.h. increasing - Rain !	
"		4.30 pm	Battalion left FORT ROMPU and occupied C Battalion billets at BOIS GRENIER & RUE DE LETTREE relieving 11th W. YORKS REGT. Zeppelin reported 9.45pm by 51st Inf. Bde. Wind S.S.W. fresh. Rain	
RUE DE LETTRE H.17,17,17,12,1/2	23.12.15		Enemy shelled B & C. Coys billets; 15 shells shrapnel time fuse. No casualties.	
"		1.15pm	Reinforcement: 2/Lt. F.L.F. REES joined Battalion. Wind S.W.-W. 20-30 m/p.h. increasing; rain	
"	24.12.15		Heavy German rifle and machine gun fire at 11pm. British Artillery fire heavy during night Wind S.S.E. light. steady. Rain, Enemy shelled vicinity of B.&.C. Coys	
"	25.12.15			

WAR DIARY or INTELLIGENCE SUMMARY

Army Form C. 2118.

Vol. V. December 1915

Place	Date	Hour	Summary of Events and Information	Remarks and references to Appendices
RUE DE LETTREE (H.17.D ½)	26.12.15		at 1.15 p.m. Casualties O.R. one killed, one wounded severely (died 26th) Wind S. changing to W. 10-30 m.p.h. rain during night 25/26th. Our artillery fired heavily 1 a.m. and 6 a.m. Battalion left billets RUE DE LETTREE and took over trenches I.31.1-5. Trenches in bad condition owing to continuous rain. Enemy quiet. Casualties: One O.R. wounded. 24th Inf. Bde on left; 25th Inf. Bde on right.	
Trenches I.31.1-2-3-4-5 (Sheet 36)	27/12/15		Wind 7.30 a.m. S. to S.W. gusty. — Weather mild — Rain during night 26/27. Enemy heavy trench guns firing water over parapet at salient (H.31.1) opposite I.31.1; towards our lines; enemy parapet visible 7.5 a.m. at even enemy but over some tobogango behind I.31.2. Casualties:— 3 O.R. wounded.	
"	28.12.15		Wind S.S.W.— Enemy parapet visible 75 m.m. gun artillery cut wire opposite I.31.5 between 12.45 p.m and 1.40 p.m destroying about 15 feet. Considerable enemy rifle and M.G. fire after dark, searching parapet and White City Road. Casualties: 2 O.R. wounded	
"	29/12/15		Wind 7.30 a.m. E. by N. steady but light. Heavy bombardment on our right at 10 a.m. 1.15 p.m. Enemy bombarded EMMA POST, STANNAY POST and ground in rear thereof with shrapnel (airburst) and whizbangs. Retaliation was asked for from C/103 which fired 12 rounds. Afterwards whizbang bombardment ceased 2.30 p.m. At 3.45 p.m. Enemy fired about 60 rounds at Bois Grenier hitting Church and houses. Casualties 1 O.R. killed; 1 wounded	

Army Form C. 2118.

WAR DIARY
or
INTELLIGENCE SUMMARY.
(Erase heading not required.)

Vol. V. December 1915.

Place	Date	Hour	Summary of Events and Information	Remarks and references to Appendices
Trenches I.31.1-2-3-4-5 Sheet 36.	30/12/15		Wind South 10.15 m.p.h. increasing during night 30/31st.	
		6.45am	Enemy fired about 35 whizzbangs on Brewery Road	
		3pm	Our heavy artillery fired at enemy trench to the right about T.I.31.1.	
		5.45pm	Our artillery fired two rounds of hostile machine gun opposite I.31.7. silencing it.	
		6.30pm	Battalion relieved in trenches by 12th D.L.I. by 2 Platoons 10th N.F. in Craters Post (8.15 pm) and by 2 Platoons 10th N.F. 7.45 pm; and took over II Battalion H.Q. LA ROLANDERIE from 11th N.F. Battalion now on our right 7th N.C.L.I. Casualties :- 1 O.R. killed.	
LA ROLANDERIE (H.11.C.5.5)	31/12/15		Wind S. to S.E. Strong. Rain. Casualties nil.	

W.T. Bierley Lt. Col.
Comdg. 13th Durham L.I.

13th Scl.
Vol: 6

Jan.

23rd

Army Form C. 2118.

Vol. 1. January 1916

WAR DIARY
or
INTELLIGENCE SUMMARY
(Erase heading not required.)

Instructions regarding War Diaries and Intelligence Summaries are contained in F. S. Regs., Part II. and the Staff Manual respectively. Title pages will be prepared in manuscript.

Place	Date	Hour	Summary of Events and Information	Remarks and references to Appendices
LA ROLANDERIE H.11.C.5.5	1.1.16		Wind S.S.W. strong	
"	2.1.16		Wind S. to S.W. 20 miles per hour, some rain.	
"	3.1.16		Wind 7.30 am S.W. warm. Battalion relieved 12th Durham Light Infantry in Trenches I.31.1-5. Trenches wet; condition of Salient at I.31.0.8.4. Very wet. Casualties 1 O.R. killed.	
Trenches I.31.1-5 Sheet 26 N.W.A.	4.1.16	7.30 am	Wind S. by S.W. Considerable hostile artillery on both flanks during morning. Our artillery made slight breach in enemy's parapet opposite I.31.1. Casualties: 1 O.R. wounded.	
		2.30 pm	Wind S.W. Enemy parapet visible 7.5 am. bright clear morning, misty in afternoon. Both sides had aeroplanes flying over lines during morning.	
"	5.1.16	7.30 am		
		7.20 am	Two pigeons crossed our line flying from direction of FLEURBAIX to LILLE.	
		10.25 am	Three pigeons observed flying from same place, same direction.	
		10.30 am	Enemy fired 72 shells at our emplacement near H.24.C.3.5 knocking out one gun; also 20 77 m.m. at BREWERY POST H.36.B.6.1½; our artillery retaliated and firing ceased. During the night enemy worked until dispersed by our M.G. fire at breach in parapet opposite I.31.1. Casualties: 2 O.R. wounded.	
"	6.1.16	7.30 am	Wind S.W. Warm. Enemy quiet during day	

2. Army Form C. 2118.

WAR DIARY
or
INTELLIGENCE SUMMARY
(Erase heading not required.)

Vol. 1. January 1916

Place	Date	Hour	Summary of Events and Information	Remarks and references to Appendices
Trenches I.31.1-5 Sheet 36 N.W.4	6.1.16		Casualties: 1 O.R. killed, 4 wounded, of which 1 at duty.	
"	7.1.16	7.30 a.m.	Wind variable S.W. to W.	
		11.30 a.m.	Trench Mortar Battery 23.2 in Salient at I.31.C.8.4 commenced firing 18 rounds. 109 Batt. R.F.A and A/105 Howitzer Batt. and B/105 (18 pdr) commenced firing on hostile gun emplacement to our front.	
		11.38 a.m.	Enemy retaliated with .77 m.m. in Salient and at BREWERY, EMMA & WHITE CITY & STANNAY POSTS.	
		12.20 pm	Enemy retaliation ceased.	
		6.20 pm	Battalion was relieved in trenches by 2nd Batt. E.LANCS REGT and proceeded to billets at HALLOBEAU (H.I.E. sheet 36) taking over from 1st WORCESTER REGT. Casualties:- 1 other ranks wounded. Weather mild.	
HALLOBEAU H.I.B. sheet 36	8.1.16	7.30 a.m.	Wind W.S.W. 30 miles per hour. Weather mild	
"	9.1.16	7.30 a.m.	Wind W.N.W. 20 miles per hour; some rain.	
"	10.1.16	7.30 a.m.	Wind N.W. to W. 5 to 10 miles per hour.	
"	11.1.16	7.30 a.m.	Wind W. to N.W. 15 miles per hour.	
"	12.1.16	7.30 a.m.	Wind S.W.	
"	13.1.16	7.30 a.m.	Wind N.W. - weather colder; some rain.	
"	14.1.16	7.30 a.m.	Wind N.W. 25 miles per hour.	
"	15.1.16	7.30 a.m.	Wind N.W. to W. 5 miles per hour.	
		3.30 pm	Battalion left billets at HALLOBEAU and proceeded to C.Batt. billets at	

Army Form C. 2118.

3.

WAR DIARY
or
~~INTELLIGENCE SUMMARY.~~
(Erase heading not required.)

Vol. 1. January 1916

Place	Date	Hour	Summary of Events and Information	Remarks and references to Appendices
Rue Marle (H.6.D.7.9.) (Sheet 36NW13)	16.1.16	7.30am	Rue Marle (H.6.D.7.9.).- Enemy shelled Armentières 10 p.m. Wind W. - 2/Lt.J.L.BAGULEY joined on transfer from 11th Durham L.I. Casualties: 1 O.R. wounded slightly.	
"	17.1.16	7.30am	Wind S.E. Rain.	
"	18.1.16	7.30am	Wind S.S.W. slight: rain during day.	
"	19.1.16	7.30am	Wind S.W. to S.S.W. Battalion took over trenches I.21.3, I.21.4, I.15.1-2 and I.16 from 12th Durham L.I. being relieved in C. Battalion by them. On our left 10th York & Lanc. Regt. (21st Div.) On Right of 68th Bde - 1st Worcester Regt. (24th Brigade) and 2nd Northamptons (24th Brigade) in "A" lines.	
		8.30pm	Heavy Artillery fire near LAVENTIE, again at 10pm and again at 2.30 a.m.: reported that enemy were attacking. Casualties: 1 O.R. killed, 1 wounded.	
Trenches I.21.3-4 I.15.1-2 I.16.	20.1.16	7.30am	Wind W. by S: fine morning; cloudy with some rain in pm.	
		9.30am	Enemy Aviatik flew over our trenches until about 10.30am.	
		10.35am	Six .77 mm. fell near Battalion H.Q. No damage.	
		1.10pm	Enemy fired 9 large calibre shells to left of CHAPELLE D'ARMENTIERES and our reserve trench at BOIS GRENIER.	
"	21.1.16	7.30am	Wind South dull day: some rain during night 20/21st	

Army Form C. 2118.

WAR DIARY
or
INTELLIGENCE SUMMARY.
(Erase heading not required)

4.

Vol. I. January 1916

Place	Date	Hour	Summary of Events and Information	Remarks and references to Appendices
—		11 a.m.	Enemy put several H.E. and Shrapnel into Trench 64 (I.15.2) and behind Trench 66 (I.16) and ARMENTIÈRES.	
		12.30 pm	A/104 and B/102 retaliated.	
		3.45 pm	Enemy shelled Battalion H.Q. at ORCHARD with 10.77 m.m. Casualties:- 3 O.R. wounded.	
Trenches:- I.21.3.4 I.15.1-2 I.16.	22.1.16	7.30 a.m.	Wind S.W. 7.30 a.m. - Dull morning.	
		9 a.m.	Enemy shelled CHAPELLE D'ARMENTIÈRES.	
		10.30 a.m.	Our 4.5 Howitzers knocked out cupola opposite I.15.2 with fourth shot. Enemy retaliating by shelling Fme de Bicz (I.15.B.2.5). Enemy cut some shrapnel into Fme de BIEZ (I.15.B.2.5).	
		12.30 pm	Our Artillery cut wire at GERMAN HOUSE I.21.B.2.1.	
		12 noon		
		2.45 pm	Trench Mortar Battery in salient fired 27 rounds at a group of 2 M.G. emplacements and 2 snipers posts at I.21.B.2½.2, knocking out both snipers plates, holing M.G. emplacement and making small breach in parapet. Enemy retaliated on our S.62 and S.63 doing little damage, but at our request A/104 and C/103 joined in doing considerable damage to their front line, S. line and communication trenches.	
		9 pm	Bright moon prevented much patrolling. Casualties:- 1 O.R. wounded.	
	23.1.16	7.30 a.m.	Wind W.	
		10 a.m.	Lt. Gen. Sir Wm Pulteney Comdg 3rd Corps visited our trenches	
		6.30 pm	Battalion handed over trenches to 12th Durham L.I. and marched to II batt.	

WAR DIARY or INTELLIGENCE SUMMARY

Army Form C. 2118.

61.I. January 1916

5.

Place	Date	Hour	Summary of Events and Information	Remarks and references to Appendices
Rue MARLE H.6.D.6.5 Sheet 36 N.W.4.	24.1.16	7.30 a.m.	Billets RUE MARLE, A Coy and 2 M.G.S. occupying Reserve trenches in BOIS GRENIER Line. Wind S.W. Light. Frost during night 23/24.	
		5.30 p.m.	A Coy and 2 M.G.S. relieved by 10th N.F.s and proceeded to RUE MARLE and SECHE RUE respectively (H.6.D.6.7 and H.5.A.3.1).	
"	25.1.16	7.30 a.m.	Wind S.W. Weather fine. Frost during night 24/25.	
"	26.1.16	7.30 a.m.	Wind S.S.W. Weather dull. Enemy shelled left Battalion left Brigade heavily during morning.	
"	27.1.16	7.30 a.m.	Wind S.W. Enemy shelled Orchard trenches and supports during morning.	
		6.45 p.m.	Battalion took over trenches from 12th DURHAM L.Inf.: B Coy 15th Royal Scots being attached to Battalion for instruction and distributed as follows D Coy on right with 2 platoons Royal Scots; C Coy centre with 1 platoon and B Coy left with 1 platoon; A Coy Bois Grenier Line in reserve.	
		11.10 p.m.	Enemy opened heavy bombardment on all trenches including one Minnenwerfer (at I.21.3) and Batts H.Q. and support trenches.	
		11.15 p.m.	Our Artillery retaliated.	
		11.20 p.m.	All guns B Group firing.	
		11.40 p.m.	Suggested to O/C B Group that fire be now lessened but they decided to carry on.	
		11.55 p.m.	Firing ceased. Casualties 2 O.R. 15th Royal Scots attached 13 D.L.I. wounded.	

Army Form C. 2118.

WAR DIARY
or
INTELLIGENCE SUMMARY
(Erase heading not required.)

Vol. 1. January 1916

Place	Date	Hour	Summary of Events and Information	Remarks and references to Appendices
Trenches I.21(3-4) I.15(1-2) I.1.16 Sheet 36.N.W.4	28.1.16	4 a.m.	Enemy shelled behind BOIS GRENIER LINE. Our heavies retaliated.	
		7.30 am	Wind W.S.W. cloudy	
		9.55 am	Enemy opened severe bombardment on all trenches and Batt'n H.Q and some minenwerfer on I.21.3	
		10.10am	Our artillery retaliated	
		10.45am	Asked O/C B Group to put on the heavies.	
		2.30 pm	Arranged scheme of defence for right company in consequence of do badly damaged state moving 1 Platoon from Reserve Coy up to S.S. line and ordering 1 Machine Gun and 2 bombers to occupy listening post.	
		4. pm	Enemy firing ceased	
		4.30 pm	Our firing ceased. Enemy machine gun enfiladed (from our left front) all places where our wire was damaged.	
		5 pm	B Coy 15th Royal Scots entered trenches and were attached as follows:— I Coy, 15th Royal Scots attached to 12th D.L.I.— "C" (centre) Coy, 1 Platoon "B" Coy left, 1 Platoon II Coy right. 2 Platoons "C" Coy. Casualties: 4 O.R. wounded, of which 1 at duty.	
	29.1.16	7.30 am	Wind 7.30 am due west.	
		12.50 pm	Enemy shelled Batt'n H.Q and I.21.3	
		1.2 pm	Our 18 pounders retaliated	

WAR DIARY or INTELLIGENCE SUMMARY

Army Form C. 2118

Vol. 1. January 1916

(Erase heading not required.)

Instructions regarding War Diaries and Intelligence Summaries are contained in F. S. Regs., Part II. and the Staff Manual respectively. Title Pages will be prepared in manuscript.

Place	Date	Hour	Summary of Events and Information	Remarks and references to Appendices
Trenches:- I.21.(3-4) I.15.1 and 2 I.16.	30.1.16	7.30 am	Asked O/C B Group for heavies	
		1.12 pm	Enemy 5.9 heavies and Minnenwerfer on and behind I.21.3	
		1.32 pm	Our 4.5's replied firing.	
		2.10 pm	Enemy whizbangs in S.I.21.3 and Bois Grenier line	
		2.24 pm	D Coy 15 Royal Scots moved to reserve line attached to 11th N.F.s	
		5.30 pm	B Coy 15 Royal Scots entered trenches and were attached as follows: 1 Platoon	
		6 p.m.	to D Co, 1 Platoon to C Coy, 2 Platoons to B Coy.	
		8.45 pm	Battalion H.Q.s moved to front line at I.15.1.	
		9.13 pm	Capt. J.A. Downey proceeded from listening post in I.15.1 with about 5 men towards German parapet; when about 460 yards from German line he was discovered but crept forward at a crawl. Three separate attempts were made to approach the point before the enemy were had been previously cut but a strong force was lying out in front of it and each time attempted to surround Capt. Downey and his party. As a surprise was impossible Captain Downey returned at 1.45 am to our trench and the attempt at a raid was abandoned. Casualties: 1 O.R. wounded.	
	30.1.16	7.30 am	Wind S.E. misty all day.	
			Enemy very quiet. B.Coy 15th Royal Scots moved to Brigade Reserve and were attached to 12th DURHAM L.I. — D Co. 15th Royal Scots reentered Trenches. Casualties: 1 O.R. wounded.	
	31.1.16	7.30 am	Wind E: clear morning.	
			Enemy very quiet.	
		6.40 pm	Battalion handed over trenches to 2nd Battalion E. LANCS and marched	

Army Form C. 2118

WAR DIARY
or
INTELLIGENCE SUMMARY
(Erase heading not required.)

Vol. 1. January 1916

Place	Date	Hour	Summary of Events and Information	Remarks and references to Appendices
			to FORTROMPU arriving in billets 9.45 pm.	

W.J. Bierrugh Lt.Col.
COMMANDING 13TH Bn. DURHAM LIGHT INFY

Army Form C. 2118

WAR DIARY
or
INTELLIGENCE SUMMARY
(Erase heading not required)

Vol. 2. February 1916

Instructions regarding War Diaries and Intelligence Summaries are contained in F.S. Regs., Part II. and the Staff Manual respectively. Title Pages will be prepared in manuscript.

Place	Date	Hour	Summary of Events and Information	Remarks and references to Appendices
FORT ROMPU	1.2.16	7.30am	Wind East	
"	2.2.16	7.30am	Wind East, cold and clear.	
"	3.2.16	7.30am	Wind East, strong, cold. — Rain during afternoon	
"	4.2.16		Weather showery in morning, dull during afternoon.	
"	5.2.16	7.30am	Wind S.W. Weather fair; fine am. Casualties 2 O.R. wounded at duty.	
"	6.2.16	7.30am	Wind S.W. Weather fine; some rain during night 5/6.	
"	7.2.16	7.30am	Wind S.W. Fine generally some showers	
"	8.2.16	7.30am	1½ Coys 11th Suffolk Regt Arrived at Fort ROMPU.	
"	9.2.16	7.30am	Wind S.E. cold, clear.	
"	"	5.30pm	Battalion relieved by 10th W. RIDING REGT. and proceeded to "C" Battalion billets RUE DE LETTREE, taking over from 9th YORKSHIRE REGT; disposition. Sheet 36 H.Q. H.17.d.1.0; A Co H.23.a.4.6; B Co H.23.C; C Co H.23.a.2.7; D Co H.29.B.2.2.	
Rue de Lettree	9.2.16	7.30am	Wind S.W.	
		3.345pm	Enemy shelled B Co billet H.23.C. "M" Coy 25th N.F.s attached to Battalion for training Casualties; 2 O.R. wounded	
"	10.2.16	7.30am	Wind west, dull	
		2/3pm	Enemy shelled LA TOULETTE [H.23 C] with about 40 Shells H.E. and Bois GRENIER LINE M. Company 25th N.F.s proceeded to A. Battalion 12th DURHAM L.I. for duty in trenches. "K" Coy 25th N.F.s joined 13th D.L.I in C. Battalion billets from 12th D.L.I.	
		7.45pm		

1875 Wt. W593/826 1,000,000 4/15 J.B.C. & A. A.D.S.S./Forms/C.2118.

Army Form C. 2118

WAR DIARY
or
INTELLIGENCE SUMMARY
(Erase heading not required.)

Vol 2. February 1916

Instructions regarding War Diaries and Intelligence Summaries are contained in F.S. Regs, Part II. and the Staff Manual respectively. Title Pages will be prepared in manuscript.

Place	Date	Hour	Summary of Events and Information	Remarks and references to Appendices
Rue de Lettree	11.2.16	7.30 a.m.	Wind S.E. Rain during night 10/11. Sleet.	
		11. a.m.	Enemy shelled ERQUINGHEM apparently aiming at the bridge; also ARMENTIERES during the afternoon.	
		7. p.m.	Battalion received reinforcement of 40 O.R. from 3rd Entrenching Battalion. "K" Coy 25th N.F⁵ moved to front line, attached to 12th N.F⁵ for instruction. "N" Coy 25th N.F⁵ joined the Batt⁵ from 11th N.F⁵ for instruction.	
"	12.2.16	7.30 a.m.	Wind N.W. morning clear.	
		1.10 p.m.	Enemy shelled Armentieres, Seale Rue, Bois Grenier and Rue de Lettree; 2 shells burst in billet at H.17, II.2.2 occupied by H.Q. A Group R.F.A. —	
		2.45 p.m.	Enemy shelled night battalion right sector trenches I.31.1-5 heavily causing 22 casualties.	
		7.45 p.m.	Battalion moved to trenches I.31.1-5 relieving 12th Batt⁵ Durham L. Inf. "N" Coy 25 N.F⁵ proceeding to trenches with the Battalion. Disposition:- "B" Coy I.31.1-2; C Coy I.31.2.3; D Coy I.31.4-5; A Coy support posts. 11th Batt⁵ Notts & Derbyshire Regt on our right. 10th Batt. N.F⁵ on our left. Casualties: 1 O.R. wounded.	
Trenches:- I.31.1-5	13.2.16	7.30 a.m.	Wind S.W.	
		9.30 a.m.	Enemy shelled Bois Grenier.	
		2.30 p.m.	Heavy hostile artillery fire on 10th N.F⁵ right trenches about I.32.	

Army Form C. 2118
3.

WAR DIARY
~~INTELLIGENCE SUMMARY~~
(Erase heading not required.)

Vol 2. February 1916

Instructions regarding War Diaries and Intelligence Summaries are contained in F.S. Regs., Part II. and the Staff Manual respectively. Title Pages will be prepared in manuscript.

Place	Date	Hour	Summary of Events and Information	Remarks and references to Appendices
	3pm	3pm	Enemy bombarded Battn. H.Q., right and centre front line trenches and the posts	
		3.15pm	O/C. II Coy. [Trench /I.31.5] reported our heavies had fired into our wire at I.31.5	
		3.38pm	A/106 Batt. R.F.A. fired about 8 rounds in retaliation. Enemy still shelling.	
		3.45pm	3 German aeroplanes over our lines	
		4.1pm	C/103 Batt. [18 pounders] fired salvo in retaliation.	
		4.5pm	C/103 Batt. [18 pounders] fired another salvo in retaliation.	
		4.10pm	Heavies fired salvo in retaliation. Enemy still firing.	
		4.15pm	Fleet of about 35 of our aeroplanes flew over our lines from the enemy.	
		4.30pm	Enemy firing ceased. Damage:- Enemy breached parapet in several places I.31.1 and in two places I.31.2; parados damaged I.31.2. Most of this damage repaired during night 13/14th.	
		6.15pm	"N" Coy. 25th N.F's left trenches and proceeded to H.Q. 12th D.L.I. Casualties:- 5 killed, 14 wounded of which 4 at duty.	
Trenches:- I.31.1-5	14.2.16	7.30am	Wind W.S.W	
		9.45am.	D Coy [I.31.5] reported working party at I.32.C.4.8	
		11.15am	Our artillery (18 pounders) fired 2 salvos H.E. at above place.	
		11.20am	Enemy shelled WHITE CITY (Battalion H.Q) with whizbangs and H.E. still about	
		11.45 am.		
		1.20 pm	Enemy shelled Bois Grenier	

WAR DIARY
~~INTELLIGENCE SUMMARY~~
(Erase heading not required.)

Army Form C. 2118

4.

Vol. 2. February 1916

Place	Date	Hour	Summary of Events and Information	Remarks and references to Appendices
Trenches I.31.1-5	15.2.16	2 pm	Rain. Received reinforcement of 19 O.R. from 23rd Inf. Base. Casualties:- 4 O.R. wounded.	
		7.30 a.m.	Wind W. by S. strong. Blizzard. Morning clear and cold.	
		2.30 am		
		2.15 pm	Enemy shelled Command Post [H.29.A.3.27 with H.E. and shrapnel and behind Balls on our right. On our front enemy quiet all day. Rain during evening and all night. Casualties ? Nil ?	
"	16.2.16	7.30 am	Wind W.S.W strong; fine morning. Enemy quiet.	
		4.30 pm	Enemy fired 8 whizbangs on I. 31.4 Casualties: 1 O.R. wounded.	
"	17.2.16	7.30 am	Wind W. strong Enemy shelled Battalion H.Q. for about an hour apparently from one gun opposite Brioux talent. Our snipers in I.31.1 hit two German snipers during the day.	
		10 am		
		7.35 pm	Battalion relieved by 12th Durham Lt. Inf. and proceeded to II Batt. billets. Disposition:- H.Q. H.11.C.6.5; A Coy H.17.C.10.1; B Coy H.11.C.10.4; C Coy H.18.C.3.6; D Coy H.18.C.6.8. 2 M.G.s at H.24 D.2.6 and 2 at Cemetery Post H.30.D.9.6. Casualties:- 1 O.R. wounded.	
La Rolanderie H.11.C.6.5 Sheet 26	18.2.16	7.30 am	Wind W; Fine clear night 17/18th, Rain all day 18th.	

Army Form C. 2118.

WAR DIARY
or
INTELLIGENCE SUMMARY
(Erase heading not required.)

Vol. 2, February 1916

Place	Date	Hour	Summary of Events and Information	Remarks and references to Appendices
LA ROLANDERIE H.11.C.6.5 Sheet 36	19.2.16	7.40am.	Wind due W. Casualty; one O.R. wounded slightly.	
"	20.2.16	7.30am.	Wind N.N.E	
		1.45 pm	Enemy shelled II Coys billet H.18.c.6.8: no casualties	
"	21.2.16	7.30am.	Wind E.	
		2.30 pm.	Enemy shelled D. Coys billet H.18.c.6.8: casualties: 1 O.R. wounded, 1 O.R. wounded at duty.	
		4 pm.	Battalion relieved in II Battalion billets by 15th Batt. Royal Scots [Lt.Col. URMSTONE Commanding) and proceeded to billets vacated by them at HALLOBEAU arriving 8.15 pm.	
HALLOBEAU Sheet 36 B.&F. G.26.9, G.2	22.2.16	7.30am.	Wind cold N.E. misty.	
	23.2.16	7.30am.	Wind N.E. cold; snowstorm almost all day.	
		10.35am.	Received wire from 68th Bn that B.E.F. would remain under command of 34th Div.	
"	24.2.16	7.30am.	Wind N. to N.E.	
"	25.2.16	7.30 a.m.	Wind E. to N.E.	
		9.30am.	Battalion moved to RUE QUESNOY, SAILLY via CROIX DU BAC and SAILLY-SUR-LA-LYS bridge relieving 22nd Batts northumberland Fusiliers (3rd Tyneside Irish) Lt.Col. A.P.Elphinstone Comdg who took over our billets at HALLOBEAU. Disposition: A Co. G.24.C.10.2; B Co G. 20. A.S.S; C Co G.24.C.10.8; D Co H.19.C.5.9; H.Q. G.24.II.10.7; Transport G.14.II.9.4.	
RUE QUESNOY	26.2.16		Weather cold: roads icy.	
		10.15am	Battalion moved to MORBECQUE sheet 36 A.II.9.C.1.7; arriving 7.35pm.	
MORBECQUE Sheet 36 A II.9.C.1.7	27.2.16		Weather slightly warmer	

Army Form C. 2118.
6.

WAR DIARY
or
INTELLIGENCE SUMMARY
(Erase heading not required.)

Vol. 2. February 1916

Place	Date	Hour	Summary of Events and Information	Remarks and references to Appendices
MORBECQUE sheet 36 A B.q.c.1.7	28.2.16	9.15 pm	Weather warmer, slush. Received orders from 68th Inf Bde that Brigade would move by train to BRUAY the following day.	
"	29.2.16		Weather cold a.m. warmer in afternoon; slight rain during evening. Battalion marched to STEENBECQUE STA, entrained 3.45 pm; detrained at CALONNE-RICOUART sheet France 36 B; marched to AUCHEL C.22.D; in billets 11.30 pm. Transport proceeded by road arriving AUCHEL at 2.30 pm.	

W.J. Bickworth LT: COL:
COMDG. 13th (SERV.) Bn. DURHAM LT. INFTY.

23 13 Dli Vol 8

Army Form C. 2118.

WAR DIARY
or
INTELLIGENCE SUMMARY
(Erase heading not required.)

Vol 3. March 1916

Place	Date	Hour	Summary of Events and Information	Remarks and references to Appendices
AUCHEL Sheet France 36 B 2nd Ed	1.3.16	7.30am	Fine am. Slight rain pm. Wind S.W.	
	2.3.16	7.30am	Wind S.E. Slight rain p.m.	
		10.52am	Enemy aeroplane dropped 3 bombs on AUCHEL	
		12.25pm	Batt'n inspected by Lt.Gen. Sir H.H.WILSON K.C.B., D.S.O. Commanding IV th Corps.	
		11 pm.	Heavy rain.	
	3.3.16	7.30am	Weather cold, dull; wind S.E. - 3.30pm snow; 7pm fine. Received reinforcement 14 men from 23rd Inf. Base Depot.	
	4.3.16	7.30am	Weather cold, snow all morning. Wind N.E.	
	5.3.16	7.30am	Weather cold. Wind N.	
	6.3.16	7.30am	Weather cold; snow night of 5/6 and morning of 6th up to 9.30 am; fine in pm. Wind N.	
	7.3.16		Weather cold am; 3pm fine. Wind 7.30 am. N.E.	
	8.3.16	7.30am	Weather cold; wind N.E. Battalion moved to billets at HERMIN Sheet 36 B 3rd Edition 7.22 D relieving Battalion of 10th French Army.	
HERMIN 7.22 D Sheet 36 II 3rd Edition	9.3.16	7.30am	Weather cold wind N.E.	
		9 am	2 Batteries 20th French Artillery passed through HERMIN	
		11.52am	2 Batt'ns Nos 268 and 290 French Infantry passed through HERMIN.	
"	10.3.16		Weather slightly warmer. Wind N.E. Arm'd snow 46th Division relieving 17th D.I. of 23rd Div.	

Army Form C. 2118.

WAR DIARY
or
INTELLIGENCE SUMMARY
(Erase heading not required.)

Vol. 3. March 1916

Place	Date	Hour	Summary of Events and Information	Remarks and references to Appendices
HERMIN P.22.D. Sheet 36B 3rd Edition	11.3.16	7.30am	Wind N.E. Weather cloudy, slightly warmer.	
		10.45pm	Received wire from 68th Inf. Bde that all moves were cancelled.	
	12.3.16	7.30am	Wind N.E. cold. - Sunshine in p.m.	
"	13.3.16		Wind almost nil southerly. Weather fine, sunshine all day. Enemy aeroplane brought down near Division H.Q. W.12. Sheet 36B.	
"	14.3.16	7.30am	Wind S.W. Weather very fine; bright sunshine all day.	
"	15.3.16	7.30am	Wind light S.W. - Weather cloudy in a.m. fine p.m.	
"	16.3.16	7.30am	Wind light S.E.	
		9.45am	Battalion left billets at HERMIN and marched via FRESNICOURT and VERDREL to COUPIGNY Q.11.C.3.8 [Sheet 36B S.E. 6th Ed] relieving 23rd London Regt. and being relieved by 21st London Regt [Lt.Col. Kennedy] both 6th Bde 47th Div.	
COUPIGNY Q.11.C.3.8. Sheet 36B.S.E 6th Edition	17.3.16	7.30am	Wind slight S.W. to S.E.	
		5.30pm	Received reinforcement of 31 B.T.R. from 16th Batt. Durham L.I.	
		6 p.m.	Batty left billets at COUPIGNY and marched via HERSIN STA. SAINS-EN-GOHELLE and BULLYGRENAY to CALONNE trenches of left Battalion Left Brigade entering from M.15.D.3.½.2.½. to M.21.A.8.7. M.Let Frame 36c. Battalion C 20000 relieving at 8.45 p.m. 17th Batt. Middlesex Regt [Lt.Col. Fenwick] and being relieved in billets by 13th Batt. Essex Regt. [Lt.Col. Pabillon].- First Division on our left, 5th Division on left 1st DIV; 10th Northumberland Fusiliers on right of Battalion.- Disposition of Battalion; Right Co 2 platoons in front line, 2 platoons in support;	

Army Form C. 2118.

WAR DIARY
or
INTELLIGENCE SUMMARY
(Erase heading not required.)

Vol. 3. March 1916

Place	Date	Hour	Summary of Events and Information	Remarks and references to Appendices
CALONNE Coy. R.E.H.Q. C.B.S. M.15.A.2.3	18.3.16	7.30 a.m.	Right centre company four platoons in front line: left centre Coy three platoons in front line one in support; left Coy three platoons in front line and one in support. Enemy quiet. Wind light S.W.	
		3.30 p.m.	Enemy fairly quiet; occasional shelling with aerial torpedoes and whizzbangs. Enemy shelled C. Coys supports M.15.A.9.2. No casualties Wind light S.W	
"	19.3.16	7.30 a.m	Enemy shelled all day; artillery retaliation practically nil. Casualties: 7. O.R wounded Wind light S.W. weather fine Enemy shelled B. Battalion area	
"	20.3.16	7.30 a.m 8.15 a.m 8.45 am 10.00 am 7.15 p.m	Enemy shelled H.Q with 59 shells and remounder of area during the day 2 Lt C Robinson B Coy discovered 6 Germans working in dry ditch opposite M.15.c. He returned to our line. A bombing party of 5 L/Cpls + 12 bombers + bayonet men was organised, who drove the Germans out of the ditch with no loss to us; a fairly successful attempt to cut off all enemy's retreat by means of M Gun rifle fire on our right + right centre Corp. A + B Coys. killing 2 men & wounding 2.	

Army Form C. 2118.

WAR DIARY
or
INTELLIGENCE SUMMARY.
(Erase heading not required.)

Vol. 3 March 1916

Place	Date	Hour	Summary of Events and Information	Remarks and references to Appendices
CALONNE M.15.A.2.3	20.3.16	9.15 p.m.	The 68th Inf Bde was asked for retaliation by the Howitzers, who supplied about 18 rounds. Casualties. 2 O.R. killed: 3 O.R. wounded of which 2 at duty.	
"	21.3.16	7.30 am	Wind S.E. clear morning	
		2 p.m.	Enemy shelled front line trenches of two right companies, A & B Coys: respectively, making two breaches in B Coys trench. Enemy used several aerial torpedoes & rifle grenades – no damage done.	
		4 p.m.	Battalion relieved by 12th Durham L. Infy. and proceeded to 'C' Bav. area. In the CALONNE SQUARE	
		9.30 p.m.	Enemy shelled 'A' Coy billet. Casualties. 1 O.R. killed. 10.R. (11th N.F.'s) killed	
		10 p.m.	No 1984 Pte. Robinson W. fell into a cellar while working on a R.E. working party. Accidentally injured – back & arm.	
CALONNE SQUARE	22.3.16	8 a.m.	Wind N.E. weather wet all day.	
		11 a.m.	Letter received from Brig. General Page Croft CMB: The Brigadier congratulates the 13th Bn. on the successful minor operation carried out on the night of the 20th/21st. – By careful organisation & determination this attack, inflicted several casualties on the enemy & suffered no losses themselves. Great credit is due to all concerned & to L/Cpl Robinson in particular for the part he played in the previous reconnaissance and in organising the attack.	
			Casualties. Pte J Simmons died of wounds inflicted 19.3.16.	
"	23.3.16	9 am.	Wind N.E. cold & wet all day.	

Army Form C. 2118.

WAR DIARY
or
INTELLIGENCE SUMMARY.
(Erase heading not required.)

Vol 3. March 1916

Place	Date	Hour	Summary of Events and Information	Remarks and references to Appendices
CALONNE SQUARE	24.3.16	3.a.m.	Started snowing and continued till evening	
		9 a.m.	Wind N.E.	
"	25.3.16	9 a.m.	Wind S.W.	
CALONNE M.15.A.2.3		5.30 p.m.	Relieved the 13th Durham Light Infy. in "B" Battalion; relief complete at 6.45 p.m.	
			Enemy very quiet	
	26.3.16	7 a.m.	Wind W.	
		9 a.m.	Enemy fired about 10 whizz bangs well behind the left centre coy. "C" Company	
		11.45 a.m.	A H.E. shell fell near a dug out in No 8 Platoon B Company	
			Casualties 2 O.R. killed 2 O.R. wounded.	
		1 p.m.	Enemy put a shell into own left company, D Company	
			Casualties 1 O.R. wounded.	
		2 p.m.	Mortar attack all mortar guns on the 68th Bde front, opened a bombardment in co-operation with Machine Guns, Rifle Grenades, and artillery against the enemy trenches between M.20.d.2.4. and M.15.d.6.9. Result was that enemy retaliated slightly on own two right companies, we suffered no losses.	
			Patrol reported that the Sap at M.15.b.8.4 was manned by 5 of the enemy-men in the sap were very quiet minded	
		10 p.m.	Wind S.E.	
			4 shrapnel shells burst over LIVERPOOL STREET.	
"	27.3.16.	7 a.m.		
		9 a.m.		

Army Form C. 2118.

Vol. 3. MARCH 1916

WAR DIARY or INTELLIGENCE SUMMARY.
(Erase heading not required.)

Place	Date	Hour	Summary of Events and Information	Remarks and references to Appendices
CALONNE M.15.a.2.3	27/3/16	11.30am	Several aerial torpedoes fell into the Left centre coy, 'C' Company	
		12.noon	Mining heard near our shaft in D coy line	
		2.30 pm	'A' Company shelled with heavy trench mortars	
		10 pm	A patrol of 3 men again went out to bomb sap at M.15.b.8.4, but found sap empty – A German rifle, loaded, was brought back from enemy mine. Wind W.	
"	28.3.16	6.30 am	9 whizzbangs fell behind 'C' Company's lines	
		8.45am		
		10.20am	20 whizzbangs fell behind right of 'C' coy wounding 17106 Pte J. Simpson who was attending to the mine.	
		11.30am	A and B Companies were very heavily shelled with trench mortars. Casualties 2 O.R. wounded	
		4 pm	Our artillery and aerial torpedoes retaliated.	
		5 pm	Mining heard at M.15.C.7.5½ and confirmed by the Tunnelling Co. Corporal	
		10 pm	Patrol again went out to bomb enemy sap at M.15.b.8.4. Two bombs were thrown into the sap – no attempt was made to enter the sap as mine was too good – not a shot of any kind was fired in retaliation. Wind W.	
"	29.3.16	6.30 am	When the billeting party was proceeding down CALONNE NORD to take over from 2nd D.L.I. a shell burst near by. Casualties 1 O.R. wounded	
		12.15 pm	Enemy sent several shells into BOYAU 10 doing a little damage	
		2 pm A.C 5pm 6 pm 6 7 pm	Several shells fell behind B Company.	

Army Form C. 2118.

WAR DIARY
or
INTELLIGENCE SUMMARY.
(Erase heading not required.)

Vol. 3 MARCH 1916

Instructions regarding War Diaries and Intelligence Summaries are contained in F. S. Regs., Part II. and the Staff Manual respectively. Title pages will be prepared in manuscript.

Place	Date	Hour	Summary of Events and Information	Remarks and references to Appendices
CALONNE M.15.a.2.3	29.3.16	5 PM	Pigeon flew over Battn. H.Q. flying in a south easterly direction	
		5.57 PM	Another pigeon flew over Battn H.Q. flying in same direction	
		8.45 PM	Battalion relieved by 12th Durham Light Infantry and proceeded to D Battalion Billets, disposition: H.Q. R.11.a.1.2, A Coy R.11.a.5.7, C Coy R.11.a.6.9, D Coy R.5.c.5.2.	
BULLY GRENAY	30.3.16	9 am	Wind NW	
		11.30 am	Flammenwerfer Demonstration held at Divisional Bombing School SAINS-EN-GOHELLE	
— " —	31.3.16	9 am	Wind W.S.W.	
		10.30 am	Enemy shelled FOSSE 10 with heavy shells and continued till 12.30 p.m.	
		5 PM	Shrapnel from anti-aircraft guns wounded 1 man slightly	

W.N. Biddulph
LT. COL:
COMDG. 13th (SERVICE) DURHAM LIGHT INFTY.

13 Durham L.I.
Vol 9
Army Form C. 2118.

13th DURHAM L.I.

WAR DIARY
or
INTELLIGENCE SUMMARY.
(Erase heading not required.)

Vol. 4. APRIL 1916

Place	Date	Hour	Summary of Events and Information	Remarks and references to Appendices
BULLY GRENAY	1.4.16	9 a.m.	Wind E	
		9.30 a.m.	Working party from D Coy, working in Cité Calonne were shelled. Casualties 1 O.R. wounded.	
		4 p.m.	Enemy brought down a FRENCH aeroplane about R.17.b & 8. both occupants being killed. Enemy artillery were very active all day & most of the night.	
"	2.4.16	9 a.m.	Wind E	
		10.45 a.m.	Enemy artillery shelled battery about R.11.2.6.	
		11.0 a.m.	Gas alarm given by CAMERONS	
		12.20 p.m.	Resumed normal condition	
		1 p.m.	Wire from Brigade reporting L.16 having been brought down	
		6.30 p.m.	Relieved 12th Battn the Durham Light Infantry in 'B' Berth area.	
		8 p.m.	Relief completed	
		8.30 p.m.	Enemy shelled heavily on our right.	
CALONNE M.15.A.2.3	3.4.16	7.30 a.m.	Wind N.E. Enemy very quiet all day	
		8.30 p.m.	Enemy shelled Pit-prop Corner M.15.C.1.1. (Sheet 36c.S.W.1.) right Company.	
		9 p.m.	18 pndrs retaliated with four salvos on enemy front line.	
		9.5 p.m.	G.O.C. 68th Bde ordered platoon in support of right Coy to stand to.	
		10.5 p.m.	Howitzers fired 50 rounds into CORNAILLES	
"	4.4.16	7.30 a.m.	Weather fine. Wind N.W. slight.	
		4.5 p.m.	Enemy shelled right Coy. Casualties: 1 O.R. killed.	

Army Form C. 2118.

2
Vol. 4. April 1916

WAR DIARY
INTELLIGENCE SUMMARY

(Erase heading not required.)

Place	Date	Hour	Summary of Events and Information	Remarks and references to Appendices
CHIONNE TRENCHES M.15.A.2.3	5.4.16	1.30am	Patrol proceeded from PIT PROP CORNER to enemy's front at M.21.A.4.7 to examine terrace in No Man's Land; Terrace unoccupied and no traces of recent work. Wind N. Weather fine.	
"		7.30am	Wind N. to N.E.	
"	6.4.16	7.20am	Enemy artillery in retaliation for our 18 pounder and howitzer fire, bombarded our front line from 12 noon to 1 pm, breaching the parapet at M.15.B.4.4 and shelling dugouts in left platoon of C. Coy about the same place; Our 18 pdrs and howitzers retaliated quickly at M.15.B.7.4 and M.15.B.9.6 with good results	
		3.30pm	Batt. relieved by 12th Batt. Durham L.I. and proceeded to "C" Batt'area. Casualties:- 3 O.R. killed. Wind light W. to N. Rain during night 6/7. - Enemy very quiet during day.	
CALONNE M.14.B.1/2.2	7.4.16	7.30am	Wind N. 18 m.p.h.	
"	8.4.16	7.30am	Enemy fired about 10 shrapnel into CALONNE; A/105 howitzer battery retaliated with about 10 shells into CORNAILLE	
"		12 noon	Casualty:- 1 O.R. accidently killed. 3rd Inf. Bde relieved 1st Inf Bde on left of 23rd Divin MAROC SECTION; 2nd MUNSTER REGT relieving 1st CAMERONS in right subsection (of MAROC SECTION) Heavy bombardment heard on left of Division.	
"	9.4.16	9 pm 7.30am	Wind N.W. slight; fine am.; misty pm. - Enemy quiet.	

Army Form C. 2118.

3.

WAR DIARY
or
INTELLIGENCE SUMMARY
(Erase heading not required.)

Vol. 4. April 1916

Place	Date	Hour	Summary of Events and Information	Remarks and references to Appendices
CALONNE M.14.B.2.2	10.4.16	7.30am	Wind N.W. light.	
		1.30pm	23rd Div. Artillery bombarded enemy front line, while Corps guns fired at hill opposite SOUCHEZ: at 4.25 pm. our bombardment became intense; at 4.30 pm artillery lifted to enemy support lines while infantry in front line fired rockets and smoke to lead the expectation being that enemy on seeing the smoke would man their parapet: at 4.35 pm all artillery again bombarded the front line. Enemy artillery retaliated throughout. Casualties: Nil.	
"	11.4.16	7.30pm	Wind N.W. rain during night 10/11.4. Battalion moved into left Battn. sector trenches, relieving 12th D.L.I. and being relieved in "C" Position by 11th Battn. N.F's. Relief completed 7.15 pm. Casualties Nil.	
CALONNE TRENCHES M.15.A.2.3	12.4.16	7.30am	Wind S.W. Rain during night 11/12.4. and all day 12.4. Enemy shelled front line with artillery and mortars throughout the day retaliation almost nil: damage: 2 M.G Emplacements hit, parapet breached near M.15.c.7.6; 2 dugouts hit; 7 trench at M.15.c.3.6. damaged and new mess dugout at M.15.c.4.4 hit	
		6 am	Casualties :- 1 O.R. killed, 3 wounded, 1 of whom at duty.	
"	13.4.16	7.30am	Wind W. 25 m/h showers Enemy again shelled front line at about M.15.c.5.3 breaching trench at that place and 50 yards to right of it Casualties nil.	

WAR DIARY
or
INTELLIGENCE SUMMARY

Army Form C. 2118.

4.

Vol 4. April 1916

Place	Date	Hour	Summary of Events and Information	Remarks and references to Appendices
TALONNE TRENCH M.15.A.1.2.3	14.4.16	7.30am	Lt. D.H. CLARKE Bt. D.L.I. having patrolled enemy re-entrant from M.15.B.8.3 to M.15.B.8.10 early this morning, continued his reconnaissance to M.15.B.8.10 reporting the presence of 3 unmarked gaps, more which first points to the conclusion that the enemy intend to push forward their line at this point.	
		9.30 pm	Wind S.W. Locally. Rain during day. Spasmodic hostile shelling during the day. 3rd Bde 1st Div. on our left had following reliefs; 2nd Munster Fusiliers relieved 1st South Wales Borderers. Casualties:- 1 O.R. wounded.	
"	15.4.16	7.30am	Wind S.W. strong; rain during night 14/15th. Batt. relieved by 12th Battn. Durham L.I. and proceeded to D Batt billets BULLYGRENAY arriving there 10.45 pm. Enemy shelled light C.Ty. constantly from 9am - 10am; at 12.45 pm and communication trench at night centre C.Ty. during the progress of the relief.	
BULLYGRENAY R.II.A.B.3 S6 & T 3b.3SE2	16.4.16	7.30am 10.55 pm	Wind W. to N.W. bright moon 15/16. Fine day 16th. French aeroplane heard over Bully Grenay.	
"	17.4.16	7.30am	Wind W. strong; rain during night 16/17th and during 17th.	
"	18.4.16	7.30am	Rain - Wind W. strong. Battalion relieved by 17th MIDDLESEX Regt. (Lt Col. FENWICK) & by 2nd Batt. Oxford & Bucks Regt. (Lt Col. A.J.F. Eden) and marched to billets at COUPIGNY (Q.11.C.4.6). Heavy rain during relief. Lt TARGET & 2/Lt. R.C. JOHNSON with 105 men C. Coy left at 3pm. and proceeded to BOUVIGNY-BOYEFFLES (Q.9.C.5.5.) attached 216th A.T.R.E.	

Army Form C. 2118.

WAR DIARY
~~INTELLIGENCE SUMMARY~~
(Erase heading not required.)

Vol. 4. April 1916. 5.

Instructions regarding War Diaries and Intelligence Summaries are contained in F. S. Regs. Part II and the Staff Manual respectively. Title pages will be prepared in manuscript.

Place	Date	Hour	Summary of Events and Information	Remarks and references to Appendices
COUPIGNY (Q.11.C.4.6)	19.4.16		Wind W. Showers during day.	
"	20.4.16		Wind W. Showers.	
"	21.4.16		Wind W. Rain in afternoon colder.	
"	22.4.16		Wind N. Rain. Received following reinforcement. 2/Lt. C.H. ROBINS, 2/Lt. H. ADAMS and 32 O.R. from 23rd Inf. Base Depot.	
"	23.4.16		Wind W. Weather very fine.	
"	24.4.16		Weather fine. Wind South. Received following reinforcement: 2/Lt. O.H. KERRIDGE and 23 O.R. from 23rd Base Depot.	
"	25.4.16		Weather fine; wind changeable—mainly Southerly light. Major URMSTON SHAW NAYLOR proceeded to NOEUX-LES-MINES to take up appointment of 2nd i/c of 6th (S) Batt. Royal Irish Rifles.	
"	26.4.16		Weather fine. very hot. Battalion relieved by 11th W.YORKS Regt. (MAJOR BARKER Comdg) and marched to BARLIN STR. entrained at 4.5.am. Arrived at 6.45 pm at PERNES. Transport proceeded by road leaving COUPIGNY 8 am.	
PERNES	27.4.16		Weather fine very hot. Wind light easterly.	
"	28.4.16		Weather fine - very hot. Wind gusty easterly	
"	29.4.16		Weather fine - Wind dusty easterly.	
"	30.4.16		Weather warm some clouds. Wind easterly.	

W. Beckwith Lt: Col:
Comdg. 13th (Serv) Bn. Durham Lt. Infty.

13. DLI
XXIII
Vol 10
Vol 5 May 1916

WAR DIARY
or
INTELLIGENCE SUMMARY.
(Erase heading not required.)

Army Form C. 2118.

Instructions regarding War Diaries and Intelligence Summaries are contained in F.S. Regs., Part II. and the Staff Manual respectively. Title pages will be prepared in manuscript.

Place	Date	Hour	Summary of Events and Information	Remarks and references to Appendices
PERNES	1.5.16		Weather fine - close - wind light	
"	2.5.16		Weather close - cloudy, rain in the afternoon. Lt OLDHAM returned	
"	3.5.16		Weather fine. Wind S.W	
"	4.5.16		Weather fine. very hot	
"	5.5.16		Weather very hot. Lt.Col. BIDDULPH went on leave and Capt. A.H.R. AUSTIN assumed command of Battalion	
		5 am	Battalion left PERNES being relieved by 10th Battn West Riding Regt. and marched to	
RECLINGHEM	6.5.16		RECLINGHEM arriving 12.40 PM	
"	7.5.16		Weather very fine early but cloudy during most of day	
"	8.5.16		Weather colder. Showery. CAPT WHITE took command of Battalion	
"	9.5.16		Weather cold. Wind W. strong. Continued showers during day	
"	10.5.16		Weather slightly warmer. Wind W.S.W. Rain all day	
"	11.5.16		Weather fine. Wind N.W	
"	12.5.16.		Weather fine - wind N.W	
"	13.5.16		Rain all day. wind W.N.W.	
"	14.5.16		Rain all day. wind W.N.W.	
"	15.5.16	11 am	Weather Drill. Battalion attended gas demonstration	
"	16.5.16		Weather dull. 2/Lt. C.T.W. SAUERBECK returned from 16th (S) Battn D.L.I.	
"	17.5.16		Weather fine. wind light N	
"	18.5.16		Weather fine wind light N.E. 2/Lt. A.G. DUGDALE arrived from 4th Special Reserve.	
"			Weather very hot wind calm. Fine all day.	
"	19.5.16.	4 am	Weather hot. light wind. Battalion left RECLINGHEM and marched to PERNES, entraining there & detraining at BARLIN and marched to billets at COUPIGNY arriving at 6 P.M.	

Army Form C. 2118.

WAR DIARY
or
INTELLIGENCE SUMMARY.
(Erase heading not required.)

Vol 5 MAY 1916

Place	Date	Hour	Summary of Events and Information	Remarks and references to Appendices
COUPIGNY	20.5.16		Weather very hot scarcely any wind. Received reinforcements of 24 O.R. from 23rd Ent. Base Depot.	
		6 P.M.	Left COUPIGNY and proceeded via BOUVIGNY, AIX NOULETTE and ARRAS Road to "B" Battalion trenches SOUCHEZ Sector, relieving 1st SHERWOOD FORESTERS.	
SOUCHEZ M.32.C.	21.5.16	5.A.M.	Relief completed 12.45 am Weather very hot, wind light SE to S.	
		3.45 P.M	Enemy shelled VIMY HEIGHTS very heavily	
		4.30 P.M	Enemy commenced firing Lachrymatory shells & attacked on a front of 1500 yards & penetrated 300 yards "G.9.c" received front Bde.	
		4.35 P.M	Lachrymatory gas drifted down on our trenches & enemy trenches on our front.	
		9.50 P.M	"S.O.S. GAS" received from 68th Inf. Bde.	
		10.30 P.M	"GAS OFF" received from Bde. AIX NOULETTE was heavily shelled during the day. Casualties 5.O.R. wounded.	
"	22.5.16	5.AM	Weather Hot Cloudy during the day	
		10.15 am	after heavy bombardment by our artillery the 47th Div. attacked VIMY HEIGHTS. Attack lasted 20-25 minutes and was repulsed. BULLY, AIX NOULETTE and CARENCY were heavily shelled. 2.O.R wounded.	
"	23.5.16		Weather dull and cooler, wind light N.W. changing to S.W.	
		6 P.M	Wind E by N. light "Gas alert"	
		4.45 P.M	Enemy fired 130 minen bombs at H.Q. Enemy shelled AIX NOULETTE all day, wrecking Coy S.S. Majors dugout and the Officers mess. Casualties 5.O.R wounded.	

Army Form C. 2118.

WAR DIARY
or
INTELLIGENCE SUMMARY.
(Erase heading not required.)

Vol 5 MAY 1916

Place	Date	Hour	Summary of Events and Information	Remarks and references to Appendices
SOUCHEZ M.32.C	24.5.16	7 am	Wind SE, slight weather dull, Rain during afternoon & evening	
		2 pm	Wind N by E	
		10 pm	Received "GAS ALERT" from the Division	
			Casualties 3 O.R. Killed and 1 O.R. wounded.	
"	25.5.16		Wind SE changing to S. Rain during day & night	
		11 am	GAS ALERT cancelled by Division	
			Casualties 1 O.R. wounded in Rear (caused by helmet)	
"	26.5.16	3.25 am	Battalion was relieved by 12th Battn. D.L.I. and proceeded to "D" Battn. position in huts in the BOIS de NOULETTE (R.27.6.8.5.5.) arriving 5.30 am	
BOIS de NOULETTE R.27.6.8.5.5			Weather fine, cool, wind W.	
			Casualties 1 O.R. wounded.	
"	27.5.16		Wind N.W. Dull & Cool	
		10.50 pm	Received S.O.S. from 1st Division, on our left.	
"	28.5.16		Wind N.E. weather fine	
		1.45 pm	Received GAS ALERT from Division	
			Weather fine. Wind N.W. by N.	
"	29.5.16		Weather dull, wind northerly. Heavy rain night of 29/30th	
"	30.5.16	8.30 pm	Battalion left BOIS de NOULETTE and relieved the 13 & (New) Battn. Durham Light Infantry in B battalion trenches M.3.2.1.2.3.4. (Capt. H.H.L. ARNOTT 2nd in Command Lines	
SOUCHEZ M.32.C.			Relief complete	
		11 pm	Tunnelling Officer reported that enemy mines were within 25 feet of our own mine R.20400 and that they were on both sides of, and aloft, our SOLFERINO, but had done no unusual damage.	

Army Form C. 2118.

WAR DIARY
or
INTELLIGENCE SUMMARY.
(Erase heading not required.)

Vol. 5 "MAY 1916"

Place	Date	Hour	Summary of Events and Information	Remarks and references to Appendices
SOUCHEZ M.32.C.	3/5/16		Wind S.W. weather fine.	
		9am	Enemy shelled near ARRAS ROAD	
		10am	Enemy shelled left of THE STRAIGHT and HUN TRENCH blocking same near SOLFERINO.	
		2 p.m.	Enemy put rifle grenades into SOLFERINO at minute intervals	
		6 p.m.	Enemy in response to our retaliation with rifle grenades and trench mortars, fired whizbangs, grenades and rum jars into SOLFERINO and the STRAIGHT	

E W White Capt
COMDG. 13th. (SERV.) Bn: DURHAM LT. INFTY.

XXIII Vol III
13 D L4/6
JUNE 1916

WAR DIARY or INTELLIGENCE SUMMARY

(Erase heading not required.)

Army Form C. 2118

Place	Date	Hour	Summary of Events and Information	Remarks and references to Appendices
SOUCHEZ 2 M.32.C.	1.6.16	7.30am	Weather fine. Wind S.W.	
		4 pm.	Our artillery opened heavy artillery fire on enemy trenches on Vimy RIDGE (that is on the right of Brigade front). Artillery fire ceased about midnight.	
		7.25pm	23rd Div. wired that O.P. on Notre Dame reported enemy standing to opposite Angres 1 and 2.	
		10 pm	Enemy put several minenwerfer into ROTTEN ROW and SEBASTOPOL. Casualties:- Lieutenant E.R.P. WOOD wounded.	
"	2.6.16	7.30am	Weather fine. Wind N.W. light.	
		3 a.m.	176 Tunnelling Coy blew camouflet in ROTTEN ROW. Mutual shelling and trench mortars throughout the day.	
		7.30pm	Our divisional artillery opened on the enemy line with 4.5's and 18 pounders for 3 minutes during which heavy trench mortars cut wire near M.32 D.0.2½	
		8.5pm	Enemy retaliated over Battn H.Q and HUN TRENCH. Casualties Nil.	
"	3.6.16	7.30am 1am.	Wind N.W. by N. light. Weather fine: night 2/3rd light with no moon. In accordance with 68th Inf Bde minor Operation Order No 58 constitutes Lieutenants D.H.CLARKE and N.H.TARGET and party of 23 men raided the enemy trench at M.32. D.0.2"½: At 1 a.m. Divisional Artillery opened an intense bombardment on enemy front line and the raiding party left our trench: at one minute past one the Artillery lifted onto enemy supports	

Army Form C. 2118

Vol. 6.

JUNE 1916

WAR DIARY
~~INTELLIGENCE SUMMARY~~
(Erase heading not required.)

Place	Date	Hour	Summary of Events and Information	Remarks and references to Appendices
SOUCHEZ 2 M. 32.C.			and the raiding party climbed over the enemy parapet and into his trenches almost without being detected.	

The Attacking party consisting of Lieutenants CLARKE and TARGET, one bayonet man and 3 bombers then turned to the left and worked about 40 yards up the trench. On that time seven Germans were disposed of in the trench, three being bayonetted and two shot while the remaining two were pushed down dugouts and bombs thrown in after them.

After working about 30 yards up the trench, the attacking party came to a step on the left into which a bomb was thrown, whereupon a German rushed out, then apparently realising that a raid was in progress, he turned back and got his rifle. He then rushed towards the attacking party and fired his rifle, but was at once shot. This party threw about 12 bombs into two deep dugouts.

By this time the first blocking party had worked about 40 yards up to the right of the point of entry and had attempted to erect a barricade. Two Germans were bayonetted in the trench in the act of coming out of dugouts. Four deep dug-outs were successfully bombed with about 45 bombs by this party. after erecting the barricade, this blocking party bombed the trench beyond.

The second blocking party remained at the point of entry and ensured the safe withdrawal of the raiding party: the Sergeant in charge shooting one German.

Owing to the wire having been cut so successfully by the 60 lb. Trench

Army Form C. 2118

Vol. 6
JUNE 1916

WAR DIARY
or
INTELLIGENCE SUMMARY

(Erase heading not required.)

Place	Date	Hour	Summary of Events and Information	Remarks and references to Appendices
SOUCHEZ M.32.C.			[Lt. J. KYLE A/23 T.M.B] at 7.30 p.m. the wiring party of 2 men specially detailed to widen the breach in the enemy in order to facilitate the return of the raiding party, had little to do.	
			The time spent in the enemy trench was about 9½ minutes and the withdrawal was carried out without any trouble from machine gun or rifle fire, which was largely due to the excellent traversing of the enemy's parapet on our flanks by our Lewis guns.	
			Our total casualties were 3 O.R. wounded.	
			Our intense bombardment of one minute drove the enemy into their dugouts thus facilitating a surprise; enemy trenches were particularly good. All the dugouts were very deep, well constructed and lit by electric light.	
		9.a.m.	Enemy shelled Battn. H.Q. for 30 min. with 5.9. Throughout the day the enemy maintained a continuous bombardment of all our trenches seriously damaging ROTTEN ROW, SEBASTOPOL, SOLFERINO, BOSCH WALK, HUN and H.Q. trench.	
		12.45 p.m	Received wire from G.O.C. 68th Infantry Bde. [B.G.65] congratulating C.O. and all ranks on the raid.	
		2.40 p.m	Received similar wire from G.O.C. 23rd Div.	
		7.30 p.m	Enemy opened intense bombardment of our front line trenches, support trenches and Battalion H.Q.: all wires were cut in the first 5 minutes: in view of the systematic gunnery of the enemy throughout the day, & the fact that the bombardment seemed to lift on to supports and communication trenches at 7.35 p.m. and that all communication with the front line was broken, the C.O. ordered the S.O.S at 7.40 p.m.: at 8.2 p.m. having ascertained from 2/Lt.	

Army Form C. 2118
Vol. 6
JUNE 1916

WAR DIARY or INTELLIGENCE SUMMARY
(Erase heading not required.)

Instructions regarding War Diaries and Intelligence Summaries are contained in F.S. Regs., Part II. and the Staff Manual respectively. Title Pages will be prepared in manuscript.

Place	Date	Hour	Summary of Events and Information	Remarks and references to Appendices
			TYSSEN in SOLFERINO SAP that the enemy had not attacked, the S.O.S was cancelled. Immediate steps were taken to repair damage caused during the day with the result that, excepting for parts of SEBASTOPOL SOLFERINO and BOSCH WALK, the damage was made good; ROTTEN ROW which was breached in 6 places being entirely repaired. Received reinforcement of 1 Officer from 3rd (Res) Batt D.L.I. 2/Lt. W.N. DAVENPORT. Casualties: - 13 O.R. wounded.	
SOUCHEZ 2	4.6.16	7.30 a.m.	Wind S.W. quiet; slight rain in evening. Enemy shelled front line with whiz bangs, rifle grenades and an occasional Minnie throughout the day	
M.32.C.		5.30 pm	Enemy opened on Batt's H.Q. and the STRAIGHT with 4.2" and 5.9" ceasing fire about 5.50 p.m.	
		9 p.m	Battalion relieved by 12th (S) Batt's D.L.I. [Lt Col. W. McGREGOR GORDON HIGHLANDERS Commanding] and proceeded by platoons to C. position [H.Q. ABLAIN ST.NAZAIRE) relieving 11th (S) Batt's Northumberland Fusiliers (Lt Col. CAFFIN Commanding] - Batt in position 12.20 a.m. Casualties: 3 O.R. wounded.	
ABLAIN-ST-NAZAIRE	5.6.16	7.30 a.m.	Wind S.W. showery. Quiet in evening. Capt. G. WHITE awarded Military Cross. L.Cpl ROBINSON awarded Military Medal. Capt White proceeded on leave & Capt A.P. AUSTIN assumed command.	
— " —	6.6.16	1 p.m.	Received reinforcement of 25 men at BERLIN. 6th Inf Bde on our right carried out relief in CARENCY section. Casualties 2 O.R. wounded; 2 O.R. wounded at duty.	

WAR DIARY

Army Form C. 2118 (5)

Vol. 6

JUNE 1916

Place	Date	Hour	Summary of Events and Information	Remarks and references to Appendices
RBLAIN-ST-NAZAIRE	7.6.16	7.30am	Wind S.W. Showery. Enemy very quiet: 11am. Enemy fired a few shells into D Coy's line at R.34.c.5.5. No damage. No casualties. – Casualties to date 201.	
"	8.6.16	7.30am	Wind W. Rain. The Battalion was relieved by 8th (S) Battn YORKSHIRE Regt [MAJOR CRANKO Worcester Regt commanding] at 11pm and proceeded to huts at COUPIGNY arriving 3.15 and 9.15 rained during the march.	
COUPIGNY Q.11.C.B.2 Sheet 36.B.S.E 6th Edition	9.6.16	7.30am	Wind W. Wet in am., fine pm. Major R.V. TURNER D.L.I arrived and assumed command of the Battalion.	
"	10.6.16	7.30am.	Wind W. Rain during night of 9/10 and all day 10th.	
"	11.6.16	7.30am	Wind W. Thundershowers during day.	
		12.15pm	Battalion left billets at COUPIGNY, entrained at BARLIN 2.35pm. and arrived PERNES 5.20 pm; being relieved in billets at COUPIGNY by 18th LONDON Regt 47th Div.	
"	12.6.16	7.30am	Weather wet wind cold W.N.W.	
		10 am	Battalion left PERNES and marched via SAINS-LES-PERNES to LISBOURG. Received draft of 75 men from 17th D.L.I.	
"	13.6.16	7.30am	Weather showery, wind W.N.W.	
		12.noon	G.O.C. 68th Inf Bde inspected the Battalion.	

Army Form C. 2118
Vol. 6
JUNE 1916

WAR DIARY or INTELLIGENCE SUMMARY

(Erase heading not required.)

Place	Date	Hour	Summary of Events and Information	Remarks and references to Appendices
LISBOURG	14.6.16	7.30am	Wind N.E. - Weather cloudy in am. fine pm.	
		11 p.m	All watches in B.E.F. advanced one hour.	
	15.6.16	7.30am	Wind N.E. -	
		9.30am	Battalion left LISBOURG and marched via BEAUMETZ to DELETTE arriving 1pm.	
			Reinforcement: 2/Lt E. THOMPSON reported his arrival from the 3rd Inf. Base Depot.	
DELETTE	16.6.16	7.30am	Wind N.E.	
	17.6.16		Weather fine. Battalion training	
	18.6.16	7.30am	Wind N.E. Weather fine.	
			Training:- Brigade in the attack	
		5.15pm	Church Parade: Lord KITCHENER memorial service.	
			Capt WHITE returned from leave and assumed the duties of 2nd in command.	
	19.6.16		Weather fair. Wind N.E.	
			Training:- Division in attack from trenches.	
			Following officers were awarded the MILITARY CROSS:- Lt. D.H.CLARKE, Lt. N.A.TARGET.	
			Following other ranks were awarded the MILITARY MEDAL:-	
			No 17190 Sgt R. BORGEY No 16121 Pte R. HEDLEY	
			22023 " R.B. WHITE " 18491 " J. KEENAN	
			17194 L-Cpl. W.A. BOWRAN " 19770 " T. MIDDLETON	
			24632 " E. HETHERINGTON " 16103 " J. MOYLE	
			16946 Pte C. BARKER " 19785 " W. ORR	
			17905 " J.T. DODDS " 28670 " A. STEPHENSON	
			20051 " W. HART " 17148 " S. WILLIAMS	

WAR DIARY or INTELLIGENCE SUMMARY

Army Form C. 2118
Vol. 6
JUNE 1916

Place	Date	Hour	Summary of Events and Information	Remarks and references to Appendices
DELETTE	20.6.16	7.30am	Weather fine. Received Reinforcements of 5 O.R.	
"	21.6.16	7.30am	Weather fine. Battalion and Brigade Exercises in Attack from Trenches. G.O.C. 23rd Div. (Maj.Gen. J.M.BABINGTON C.B. C.M.G) presented the ribbon of the Military Cross to 3 Officers and the ribbon of the Military Medal to 13 N.C.O's and men.	
"	22.6.16	7.30am	Weather hot. Field Operations: Brigade in the attack from trenches. Received following Reinforcement from 17th D.L.I.:- 2/Lt. J.C. BATTY, 2/Lt. H.R. WHEATLEY, 2/Lt. G. WHARTON.	
"	23.6.16	7.30am	Weather dull, hot; thunder showers during day. Wind S. Received following Re-inforcement:- 2/Lt. W.L. OAKES from 23rd (S) Batt. D.L.I.; 2/Lt. W. THOMPSON, 2/Lt. J. DAWSON and 2/Lt. C.L. BROWN all from 17th (S) Batt. D.L.I.	
"	24.6.16	7.30am	Weather dull, showery; rain all night 23/24th. Batt: left DELETTE 8 am. (transport 7am.) and marched via HAMETZ to AIRE; entrained and left 1.26 pm; arrived LONGEAU STA. 8.40 pm. via ST. POL, DOULLENS, PICQUINY, AMIENS. Left LONGUEAU STA. 9.35 am. and marched to PICQUIGNY arriving 3.30 am. 25th. Casualties on march: 2/Lt.HARRAMS and 2 O.R. admitted MIDLAND F.A. AMIENS. 23rd Div came under orders of 2nd Corps, IVth (Reserve) Army.	

Army Form C. 2118

Vol. 6
JUNE 1916.

WAR DIARY
or
INTELLIGENCE SUMMARY
(Erase heading not required.)

Instructions regarding War Diaries and Intelligence Summaries are contained in F. S. Regs., Part II. and the Staff Manual respectively. Title Pages will be prepared in manuscript.

Place	Date	Hour	Summary of Events and Information	Remarks and references to Appendices
PICQUIGNY	25.6.16		Weather wet, heavy rain forecast night of 25/26th.	
"	26.6.16		Weather wet heavy rain p.m. and night of 26/27th.	
"	27.6.16	8 p.m.	Weather showery. 2nd (Indian) Cavalry Div. began to pass through PICQUIGNY on way to Front	
"	28.6.16		finished passing 5 a.m. 28th. Weather wet; rained all morning.	
"	29.6.16		Weather cloudy a.m. G.O.C. 23rd Div. (Maj. Gen. J.M. BABBINGTON C.B, C.M.G.) presented ribbon of Military Medal to Pr/On. No. 15336 Pte T.F. GOWLAND and No. 17112 Pte J.W. JEFFERS.	
"	30.6.16	7.30 a.m.	Weather fine: hot in p.m. Battalion left billets in PICQUIGNY and marched to ALLONVILLE via	
	2.52 p.m.		AILLY-SUR-SOMME, ARGOEUVES, LONGPRE and POULAINVILLE arriving ALLONVILLE 7.40 p.m. Dist. 12 miles - no casualties.	

R.B. Turner Major
Lt.-Col.
COMDG. 13th (SERV.) Bn. DURHAM LT. INFTY.

68th Bde.
23rd Div.

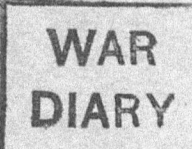

Brigade temporarily under orders of 34th Division 16th to 20th July.

13th BATTALION.

DURHAM LIGHT INFANTRY.

JULY 1916

WAR DIARY
INTELLIGENCE SUMMARY
(Erase heading not required.)

JULY 1916

Place	Date	Hour	Summary of Events and Information	Remarks and references to Appendices
ALLONVILLE	1.7.16		Weather fine: Sunshine.	
		8.32 pm	Battalion left ALLONVILLE and marched to FRANVILLERS via QUERRIEU, PONT NOYELLES and LA HOUSSOYE (on Amiens-Albert road) to FRANVILLERS arriving 12.40 am. 2.7.16. Casualties nil. The whole of 68th Inf Bde, 70th F.A. and 68/1st M.G. Coy in FRANVILLERS	
"	2.7.16		Weather fine.	
		9.30 pm	Battalion left billets at FRANVILLERS and marched to bivouacs at MILLENCOURT arriving midnight. Casualty:- 1 O.R killed	
"	3.7.16		Weather fine, very hot	
		6.30 pm	Battalion left bivouacs at MILLENCOURT and marched to bivouacs at E.9 sheet 62D first edition (40000) S.W. of Albert, arriving 8 pm.	
E.9 Sheet 62D	4.7.16		Weather close and rain all night 3rd/4th	
ALBERT		2.30 pm	Heavy rain. Battalion left trenches at E.9 in rear of Brigade and arrived BECOURT WOOD 3.20 pm.	
		3.45 pm	Conference at Becourt Chateau (68th Inf Bde H.Q.) - Major Gen. Babington considered too many troops in BECOURT WOOD; 13th D.L.I and 10th N.F.S ordered to return to bivouacs at E.9.	
		4.45 pm	Battalion left BECOURT WOOD, arrived E.9 5.30 pm.	
"	5.7.16		Damp - clearing	
"	6.7.16	10 am	Battalion moved from ALBERT to BECOURT WOOD.	
"	7.7.16	4.30 pm	Ordered to relieve line of 68th Inf Bde. Detailed 2 Coys to relieve 12th D.L.I. and 2 Coys	

WAR DIARY or INTELLIGENCE SUMMARY

Army Form C. 2118.
Vol. 7 Page 2.
JULY 1916

Place	Date	Hour	Summary of Events and Information	Remarks and references to Appendices
			11th N.F.- Subsequently owing to alteration in situation received orders from Brigadier to relieve 11th N.F. on line X.16.c.3.0 - X.15.d.0.0 and to consult on spot as to disposition of remainder of Battalion. By the time the Battalion got to SCOTS REDOUBT, the trenches were waist high in mud and movement at all was next to impossible. After consultation I found the line was not as expected and that 11th N.F.s were not holding the line as above. Guides owing to the mixed condition of affairs, had no idea of where to guide one Company alone reached its destination properly, the difficulty of movement and pitch darkness being a great hindrance. The approximate position attained was:- X.22.A.3.4.- X.21.B.5.6 - X.21.B.6.9 also X.15.D.5.1- X.15.D.2.5 and Support Company X.21.B.5.6 - X.21.B.3.8. - One Company 10th N.F. X.15.D.5.1 - X.15.D.8.0. - One Company 12th D.L.I. X.16.C.1.2 - X.16.C.3.0. Casualties nil. Weather dull.	
	8.7.16		During the day it was attempted to get the line into that which appeared to be necessary. Movement however was (still next to impossible and difficult to attain by daylight without undue loss. One of our patrols reported the enemy to be in BAILIFF WOOD (4.20 pm). About 5 pm. two Companies commenced to move up to attack Brigade objective. They were however heavily barraged and machine guns were turned on them. The Brigade on the right had failed to get forward and I received orders from 68th Bde to hold up attack, which was done. At the same time a patrol under Lt TARGET entered the German trench X.16.D.2.4 and proceeded northwards	

WAR DIARY or INTELLIGENCE SUMMARY

Army Form C. 2118.
Vol. 7
JULY 1916
Page 3.

Place	Date	Hour	Summary of Events and Information	Remarks and references to Appendices
	9.7.16		they saw about 40 Germans about X.16.B.2.3 Casualties:- 2/Lt. H.R. WHEATLEY wounded; O.R. 4 killed, 18 wounded, 3 wounded at duty, 3 missing. Weather dull; slight rain. During the night of the 8/9th the Battalion got into position as follows:- X.22.A.3.4 – X.21.B.9.9 and X.16.C.1.7 – X.16.C.1.2 and X.15.B.8.0 – X.16.B.5.6. During the early hours of the morning this was further improved until my position was X.22.A.3.4 – X.21.B.9.9 – X.16.C.1.2 – X.16.A.1.3. There were some slight movements on my left at times to keep touch with the Brigade on my left, but the above was my line practically, for the remainder of the time. Under orders from 68th Inf. Bde. I sent a bombing party along the French X.16.R.1.3 – X.16.A.7.4. This party mistook the French and followed some leading into BAILIFF WOOD where on arrival they came under our shell fire and a machine gun of the Germans. Capt. PEASE, 12th D.L.I. during the evening established himself along the French X.16.A.1.3 – X.16.A.3.4 and also X.16.A.1.3 – X.16.A.1.4 – X.15.B.8.5. Casualties:- 2/Lt. KERRIDGE wounded; O.R. 4 killed, 60 wounded, 7 wounded at duty, 6 wounded shell-shock, 2 missing.	
	10.7.16		At 4.30 p.m. the attack of the 69th Bde passed through the lines of the Battalion and took CONTALMAISON taking up a line X.16.A.1.3 – X.16.B.2.5 on my left. As there had become a gap from X.16.A.1.3 – X.16.A.1.4 – X.15.B.8.5 two of my left platoons (A Co) were moved up into it; the remainder of my frontage shaking out to the left to hold the original frontage. The strong party detailed to block X.16.A.2.6.- 2.7 by the Bde. was not required, and so advised YORKSHIRE REGT. to consolidate until I ordered their return.	

WAR DIARY
INTELLIGENCE SUMMARY

Army Form C. 2118.

Vol. 7.
JULY 1916

Place	Date	Hour	Summary of Events and Information	Remarks and references to Appendices
	11.7.16		The Battalion was relieved by 1st CAMERON HIGHLANDERS [Lt.Col. E CRAIG-BROWN D.S.O. (Condg.)], 1st Brigade, 1st Division at 5.40 a.m. On the 11th and marched to billets in ALBERT. Casualties:- Capt. G.M.LONG, 2/Lt. G. WHARTON, 2/Lt. A.GREEN wounded; O.R. 6 killed, 45 wounded, 3 wounded at duty, 1 wounded shell-shock, 3 missing. Weather fine.	
		5.40 a.m	Battalion marched by Coys after relief to billets in ALBERT arriving 8.30 a.m; and became attached to 34th Div.	
ALBERT	12.7.16		Weather fine. Enemy shelled ALBERT 5 p.m, 7 p.m and 11.15 p.m. Casualties:- 2 O.R. wounded. Received following telegram from G.O.C. IVth Army through 68th Inf. Bde: "B.M. 116 dated 12.7.16. Following from 3rd Corps begins AAA. Following from Genl. "RAWLINSON begins AAA Please convey to 23rd Div. Any hearty congratulations "on their capture of CONTALMAISON AAA They have acquitted themselves right "well and I desire to thank them most heartily for their gallantry and "the fine fighting spirit displayed by all ranks AAA Ends AAA."	
"	13.7.16		Weather dull, some rain. Enemy shelled ALBERT during the day. Battalion under 3 hours notice to move from 2 p.m.	
"	14.7.16		Weather dull, some rain. Battn. received order to move at ½ an hours notice.	
"		4 p.m.	Battn. moved to Rue de PERONNE, ALBERT.	
"	15.7.16	3.30 a.m	Received 68th Inf. Bde. Operation Order No. 37. 68th Bde. would act in support	

WAR DIARY
INTELLIGENCE SUMMARY
(Erase heading not required.)

Army Form C. 2118.
Vol. 7
JULY 1916

Place	Date	Hour	Summary of Events and Information	Remarks and references to Appendices
	16.7.16	7.30 a.m.	in support of 34th Division operations against POZIERES. Battalion left billets in ALBERT and moved to support trenches; A & B Coys occupying trenches X.15.B.7.2 - X.16.B.2.5 and X.15.B.8.1 - X.15.D.2.5. Headquarters and remaining two Companies in HELIGOLAND X.21.C.1.7. Casualties nil. 34th Div. attack failed.	
		2.30 p.m.	Weather fine am; rain pm. 66th Inf. Bde. relieved 112th Inf. Bde, 34th Div. - Battalion moved to new trenches	
		4.30 p.m.	2.30pm, relieving 6th Bedfordshire Regt. Batts HQ in Sausage Valley near Gordon Dump; 3 Platoons D Coy occupying posts near CONTALMAISON WOOD and X.16.A.2.8; C Coy providing digging party of 125 men to assist in consolidating front line held by 12th D.L.I. An attempt by a bombing party under 2/Lt BROWN to block and hold trench at X.5.C.4.3 between 68th Bde and 1st Div. failed.	
			Casualties:- O.R. 3 wounded one missing.	
	17.7.16		Weather dull.	
near POZIERES		10 a.m.	68th Inf. Bde. formed smoke barrage on enemy front S.W. of POZIERES	
		8. p.m.	12th & 2.L.I. after intense bombardment attacked enemys trench S. of POZIERES on front X.4.D.8.2 - Bapaume - Albert road but were unable to effect an entry in enemy trench; enemy placing artillery barrage in front of their line at 7.50 pm.	
		10 p.m.	Disposition of 13th D.L.I. as follows:- A Co X.11.A.6.0 X.10.B.9.7; B Co X.10.B.9.7 - X.10.B.17; C Co X.10.B.17 - round N. of wood to X.4.C.3.1; D Co (in support) X.16.A.1.7 to X.10.C.11 and posts; Batts HQ X.16.A.14.	
		10.50 p.m.	The 10th N.F. having been ordered to relieve 12th D.L.I in captured enemy trench were to attack POZIERES at 3.30 am. 18th inf: owing to failure of 12th D.L.I. to occupy	

Army Form C. 2118.
page 6
Vol. 7
JULY 1916

WAR DIARY
or
INTELLIGENCE SUMMARY
(Erase heading not required.)

Place	Date	Hour	Summary of Events and Information	Remarks and references to Appendices
			enemy trench this operation was postponed and 68th Bde issued following orders at 10.25 pm 17.7.16:- "The 12th D.L.I. have not succeeded. The 10th N.F. will take over the line originally held by 12th D.L.I. from the left to the French 53-17 including posts in front of "the line. 13th D.L.I. will hold with three Companies from the right of the 10th N.F. to the right of the original line of the 12th D.L.I. and posts in front AAA 13th D.L.I. will withdraw from the N.W. of French A.7.5 to B.1.7 and will reoccupy their "advanced positions" of this morning about 10 B near CHALK PIT AAA 13th D.L.I. will make way at once for 10th AAA 12th D.L.I. will not evacuate until relief is complete when they will march back to 11th N.F. trenches AAA 11th N.F. will occupy line of 15 B.7.2 - 16 B.2.5 and area."	
			Casualties:- O.R. 19 wounded, 3 wounded at duty.	
near POZIERES	18.7.16	6 a.m.	Weather dull. Disposition 13th D.L.I. as follows:- A Co X.11.A.3.5 to X.10.B.8.6; B Co X.10.B.8.6 to X.10.B.1.7; C Co X.16.A.1.3; D Co in posts near CHALK PIT	
		2 p.m.	Ordered A.Co to relieve Company of 12th D.L.I. during the evening. Furnished guides to 68th Inf Bde H.Q. for parties of 1st Div. and 11th N.Fs for digging trenches from X.10.B.9.7 and from X.11.A.2.3. Received following reinforcements - at transport field:- 2/Lt. G.P. GRAY from 23rd D.L.I.; 14 O.R. and 11 O.R. from Cheshire Regt, E.Yorks & 18th D.L.I. Casualties; 2/Lt. E. THOMPSON wounded; O.R. 5 killed, 24 wounded, 1 wounded at duty, 2 wounded shock shell.	
	19.7.16		Weather fine.	

WAR DIARY

Army Form C. 2118.
Page 7.
Vol. 7.

JULY 1916

Place	Date	Hour	Summary of Events and Information	Remarks and references to Appendices
near POZIERES	20.7.16	4.15 a.m.	Ordered C. Co. to occupy new trench from point X.11.A.2.3.	
		6. a.m.	Disposition of Battn. now as follows:- Continuous line from approximately X.10.B.0.5 - X.10.B.9.7 - X.11.A.2.5 - X.11.A.4.6. also X.11.A.8.8 along road. One Company X.9.D.9.0 to X.9.D.7.6 with posts at X.10.A.7.1 X.10.C.6.3 and X.10.C.8.4; not in touch with Division on right. Casualties:- O.R. 1 Killed; 10 wounded. Weather fine. Heavy enemy artillery fire all night on Battn. H.Q. crossroads at X.16.A.1.2 & Sausage Valley; enemy using large amount of gas shells.	
		3 a.m.	Battalion relieved by 1st and 3rd Anzac Bde and marched to bivouacs at ALBERT, H.Q. arriving ALBERT 6.30 a.m.	
		1.15 p.m.	Battalion marched to billets in FRANVILLERS arriving 4.55 p.m. Casualties:- O.R. 3 wounded. Weather fine.	
FRANVILLERS	21.7.16		G.O.C. 23rd Div. presented the ribbon of the Military Medal to No. 15 Sgt. No. 24775 Pte. W. HUTCHINSON 18170 Sgt. T. FITZPATRICK 17108 Pte. T. SUDDES Received following reinforcement from 37th Infantry Base Depot; 56 O.R. of Yorks Regt.	
"	22.7.16		Weather dull cloudy. Received draft from 77 O.R. of 21st N.F. Brigade in reserve to Dist. and 19th Div. from midnight 22/23 and ready to move.	

WAR DIARY or INTELLIGENCE SUMMARY

Army Form C. 2118.
page 8
Vol. 8
JULY 1916

(Erase heading not required.)

Place	Date	Hour	Summary of Events and Information	Remarks and references to Appendices
FRANVILLERS	23.7.16		at one hour's notice while above Divisions attack towards MARTINPUICH.	
		10 am	Attack failed. Brigade no longer in reserve.	
			Weather dull.	
			Received draft from 31st Infantry Base Depot of 65 O.R. of 16th, 20th and 26th N.F.'s	
"	24.7.16		Weather dull. warm	
"	25.7.16		Weather dull.	
		11:30 am	68th Infantry Bde inspected by Lieut-Gen Sir William Pulteney Comdg IIIrd Corps.	
"	26.7.16	9 am	Battalion left FRANVILLERS via ALBERT-AMIENS road; halted at ALBERT from 12 noon to 5 pm: and relieved 2nd Royal MUNSTER FUSILIERS (Lt.Col. LYONS Comdg) in trenches at CONTALMAISON at 8pm: disposition of Battalion:—	support
			H.Q. and A Coy X.17.C.1.9 ; B.C. & D Coys from X.17.B.a.4. to X.16.B.1.5. (in front line.) 1st Australian Div. on left ; 9th York and Lancs Regt on right	1st
			Casualties :- O.R. 4 wounded.	
			Weather fine	
CONTALMAISON	27.7.16	1:30 am	Reported that enemy had attacked MUNSTER ALLEY as far as point 41 from 10th N.F.	
		5 am	Enemy bombarded front line.	
		11:15 am	10th N.F. reported having taken MUNSTER ALLEY up to point 94 and were consolidating. CONTALMAISON shelled on and off all day.	
		9:25 pm	Battalion relieved 10th N.F. (Lt Col. R. MANNER'S Comdg) disposition:— Right Coy with right on MARTINPUICH Rd: centre Coy with right at junction of GLOSTER ALLEY and Old German trench 2 and with left 30 yards from junction of SUSSEX trench and O.G.2; Left Coy two platoons in front line with left on support point 78 and right on centre communication. Two platoons left Coy and H.Q bombers	

Army Form C. 2118.
Vol 8 JULY 1916
page 9

WAR DIARY
or
INTELLIGENCE SUMMARY
(Erase heading not required.)

1000f

Place	Date	Hour	Summary of Events and Information	Remarks and references to Appendices
NEAR POZIERES H.Q. at X.11.B.9.7 28.7.16		10 pm	at bombing post in MUNSTER ALLEY point 41. Support Cy in O.G.1 and H.Q. at X.11.B.9.7 Lt. BUTTERWORTH with A Cy and one Cy of 12th D.L.I. advanced the French from X.6.C.8.5 in a N.W. direction and parallel with German switch line running from S.1.C.2.9 to MUNSTER ALLEY.	
		3.30 am	French dug for 200 yards and held by 2 platoons A Cy Casualties :- Lieut. G.S. KAYE-BUTTERWORTH wounded at duty; O.R. 6 wounded; 1 wounded at duty; 1 wounded self inflicted accidental; 2 wounded shock shell.	
			Weather dull, hot.	
		4.15 am	Lt. SAVERBECK reported that he had pushed up MUNSTER ALLEY for distance of 70 yards from point 41 and was consolidating and blocking. Enemy bombed Lt. SAVERBECK out of MUNSTER ALLEY; partly being forced back to point 41.	
		7.44 am		
		8.E am	Lt. SAVERBECK wounded, 2/Lt. O'CALLAGHAN taking command at point 41.	
		8.20 am	2/Lt O'CALLAGHAN was wounded and C.S.M. MORTON 13th D.L.I. took command at point 41. Sgt. CARLING with Lewis rifle near point 41 kept back any of the enemy who attempted to cross Lt SAVERBECK's former block.	
		8.25 am	Enemy abandoned their attack.	
		10.20 am	2/Lt JOHNSON and all bombers C. Cy sent to point 41 with 2/Lt ROBINS	
		3 pm	Lt TARGET patrolled MUNSTER ALLEY from point 41. reported he could gain up to 100 yards with artillery co-operation	
		5.20 pm	G.O.C. 68th Inf Bde ordered by phone that part of MUNSTER ALLEY facing N.W. should be consolidated; this was done before completion of relief.	
		5.35 pm	Lt TARGET reported enemy heard talking behind first block in MUNSTER ALLEY to be 50 yards from our block; enemy heard talking behind block; block was bombed and our left barricade	

WAR DIARY or INTELLIGENCE SUMMARY

Army Form C. 2118.
page 10
Vol 8 JULY 1916

Place	Date	Hour	Summary of Events and Information	Remarks and references to Appendices
		6.45 pm	pushed forward a further 10 yards to a better position. On enquiring received following from O/C. ANZACS on my left :- "This Division is attacking German positions N and N.E. of POZIERES - O.G.1 from MARTINPUICH 1/20000 - O.G.2 from X.5.B.4.1 and N.E. to R.34 A.9½. Ref sheet 57 D S.E.4 M.000 (OVILLERS) "MARTINPUICH 1/20000. We will endeavour to link up with you at X.5.B.4.1 and will send ammunition up O.G.2 if we consolidate. Time to be notified later."	
		9 pm	All Companies relieved by 10th W. RIDINGS, 69th Inf Bde. excepting bombing post of B Co at point 0.5. This relieved 1.30 am 29/7.	
		9.30 pm	Enemy bombarded O.G.1 and wounded 2/Lt ROBINS, DUGDALE and CHARLTON	
		9.45 pm	Heavy bombardment on our right by enemy	
		12 midt	ANZACS attacked on our left after heavy bombardment. Casualties L/C. T.W. SAUERBECK, 2/Lt. O.T. O'CALLAGHAN, W.G. CHARLTON, C.H. ROBINS, R.G. DUGDALE wounded: O.R. 7 killed, 32 wounded, 1 at duty, 2 self inflicted accidental, 5 shock shell. 2 missing.	
ALBERT	29.7.16	5.30 am	Weather fine, hot. Battn arrived in billets Rue Bapaume	
		9.30 am	G.O.C. 23rd Div. presented ribbon of Military Medal to No 22611 Sgt. W.A. SMITH D Co	
	30.7.16		Weather fine, hot Lt. Col. R.V. TURNER admitted 23rd Div. Rest Camp BRAISIEUX. Capt. G. WHITE assumed command of Battalion.	
	31.7.16		Weather fine, hot	

G White
Lt-Col Capt.
Comdg. 13th (SERV.) Bn. DURHAM LT. INFTY.

68th Brigade.
23rd Division.

1/13th BATTALION

DURHAM LIGHT INFANTRY

AUGUST 1 9 1 6

Army Form C. 2118.

WAR DIARY
or
INTELLIGENCE SUMMARY.

Vol. 8. Page 1.

(Erase heading not required.)

AUGUST 1916. 13. D.L.I. Vol 13

Place	Date	Hour	Summary of Events and Information	Remarks and references to Appendices
ALBERT	1.8.16		Weather hot.	
		3 p.m.	Battalion left billets in ALBERT 3 p.m. Landing over to 10th W. RIDINGS and marched to PEAKE WOOD relieving 8th YORKS REGT. Lt Col VAUGHAN commanding. Relief complete 5-10 p.m.	
		11.55 p.m.	Heavy British bombardment about point X.5.B.4.1. MUNSTER ALLEY. Casualties: Killed self-inflicted 1 O.R. Wounded 4 O.R.	
NEAR CONTALMAISON	2.8.16		Weather hot. Fine.	
		3 p.m.	Usual enemy bombardment.	
		3 p.m.	Our artillery bombarded enemy switch line till 3.30 p.m.	
		5 p.m.	Battalion moved to front line relieving 9th YORKS REGT. who marched to PEAKE WOOD after relief. Relief complete 7 p.m. Disposition. Four Coys in front line :- Right Coy: A. Coy from S.1.C.O.6. and post at S.1.C.2.7. 16.X.6.D.8.7. and down GLOSTER ALLEY. Right Centre Coy: C. Coy: BUTTERWORTH TRENCH from junction with LANCS TRENCH at X.6.D.8.4. to X.6.C.1.8. Left Centre Coy: B. Coy. X.6.C.1.8 to point X.5.D.7.8 and hence 16.X.5.D.4.1. Left Coy: X.5.B.4.1. and post in MUNSTER ALLEY 16.X.5.B.2.1. Headquarters at X.11.B.9.7. 11th Australian Regt (Lt. Col Martin commanding) on left. Sherwood Foresters (90th Bde.) on right.	

WAR DIARY or INTELLIGENCE SUMMARY

Army Form C. 2118.

Vol. 8 Page 2.

AUGUST 1916

Place	Date	Hour	Summary of Events and Information	Remarks and references to Appendices
NEAR CONTALMAISON	3.8.16		Casualties: Wounded 1 O.R. Weather fine. During the night 2/3rds. assisted by working parties aggregating 210 from 10th N.F. the line from GLOSTER ALLEY on right was deepened and fire-stepped including deepening GLOSTER ALLEY and BUTTERWORTH TRENCH, sap continuing for 70 yards from BUTTERWORTH TRENCH at about X.6.C.5.6. towards enemy line dug from X.6.C.18 to X.5.D.7.8. trench in O.G.1. repaired and tank post in MUNSTER ALLEY strengthened and wired all by 4 a.m.	
		9 a.m.	Heavy bombardment on right. 12th D.L.I. attacking. Received wire from 68th Bde. S.C. 131. that Div. state Germans preparing to attack with gas.	3
		9:30 a.m.	Received wire from 68th Inf. Bde. that 2/Yorks. 10th N.F. would hold O.G.2.	
		12:45 p.m.	One platoon 10th N.F. in position in O.G.2. Second lost its way arriving 2:30 p.m.	
		6:20 p.m.	Battalion relieved by 10th N.F. Lt. Col. Lord R. Manners commanding and proceeded to Billets near CONTALMAISON. Throughout the day our artillery shells fell short mainly in MUNSTER ALLEY.	
		5:15 p.m.	O/6 D Boy reports he had been compelled to evacuate MUNSTER ALLEY post in consequence. 10th N.F. took over this post but were compelled to evacuate it for the same reason for a time.	
		10:20 p.m.	Received S.O.S. Vcos from 51st Div. on Regt. of Aygees on our left. Casualties:- 2/Lt. T.E. SAINT wounded O.R. 6 killed, 14 wounded, 1 wounded at duty, 1 self-inflicted wound and 6 shell shock.	

WAR DIARY or INTELLIGENCE SUMMARY

Army Form C. 2118.
Vol. 8. Page 3.

AUGUST 1916

Place	Date	Hour	Summary of Events and Information	Remarks and references to Appendices
NEAR CONTALMAISON	4.8.16	3:00 pm	Weather fine. Battalion relieved 16th Trenches and relieved 10th N.F. Disposition :— R. Coy. BUTTERWORTH TRENCH D. Coy. NEW TRENCH B. Coy. from Point X.5.B.4.1. to O.G.1. C. Coy. and C. Coy. 10th N.F. in O.G.2. B. Coy. 10th N.F. GLOSTER ALLEY to BUTTERWORTH TRENCH Attack on TORR TRENCH and point 73. Objective X.5.B.9.4. to X.5.B.5.3:— In accordance with 68th Inf. Bde. Operation Order 44 the first attacking wave left NEW trench at 9:15 pm 4.8.16 and were immediately replied with Machine gun and rifle fire from TORR TRENCH and M.G. fire from behind the barricade in MUNSTER ALLEY. After crossing MUNSTER ALLEY the smoke barrage put up by the ANZACS still further confused matters. The second wave followed 650 yards behind the first and some few men under Captain AUSTIN got into TORR TRENCH where a bomb fight remained in progress up to about 2:15 am. After the second wave crossed MUNSTER ALLEY a string bombing party bombed up MUNSTER ALLEY for a distance of about 60 yards where they were stopped by a block which was wired. Held by the enemy and supported by a Machine Gun about 40 yards S.W. of Point 73. Here a block was made from which we were later compelled to fall back a few yards when block. Another block was made and held about 18 yards from the enemy block. At 12:30 am 5th personally went up to Point 41 to look over the situation with a view to another attack on TORR TRENCH. Owing to the wakefulness of the enemy, the enfilade machine gun fire from up MUNSTER ALLEY and the	4

WAR DIARY or INTELLIGENCE SUMMARY

Vol. 8. Page 4.
Army Form C. 2118.

AUGUST 1916.

Place	Date	Hour	Summary of Events and Information	Remarks and references to Appendices
			unlikelihood of new troops being able to cross MUNSTER ALLEY (where I know already had a stiff bomb fight) on my flanks) and reach their objective without becoming disorganised, I decided against another attack and confined my attention to a bombing assault round the enemy block in MUNSTER TRENCH under Lt. TARGET.	
			At 2.20 am. I was informed the attack had failed Lt TARGET and most of his men having been killed. Reinforcements were at once collected by Lt. CLARK on the spot and sent up MUNSTER ALLEY.	
			At about 3.15 am. most of these reinforcements having become casualties, I again sent about 20 men up MUNSTER ALLEY to hold our block. This party was relieved at about 9 am. by an officer and 25 bombers of 10th N.F. when bombing had practically ceased on both sides.	
			NOTE:- North of point 93 MUNSTER ALLEY was not blocked by our artillery except shrapnel and was seen to be full of German troops during the afternoon & evening.	
	9.25 pm		All telephone wires working	
	9.15 pm		Intense bombardment of BAFF TRENCH by our artillery	
	9.20 pm		First wave advanced out of assembly "NEW" trench.	
	9.22 pm		Second wave advanced out of assembly trench to objective.	
	9.32 pm		Received phone message from 2nd Lt. ROBINSON D.Coy.: "We're relieved."	
	9.33 pm		Received phone message from Lt. CLARK "B. Coy are going forward."	
			When the first two waves of D. Coy crumpled up Lt. CLARKE collected the remnants and met his company and ordered them up in support and at once instructed bombers to work up MUNSTER ALLEY	
	11 pm		Received following message from Lt. CLARKE:- "D. Coy retired and so I sent B. Coy were forward and immediately bombing to work up Munster Alley and Recce reports they have got well into trench so have sent bombing party from C.Coy to reinforce them. Why D.Coy retired God knows. I got them to go forward again without success."	5.

WAR DIARY or INTELLIGENCE SUMMARY

Army Form C. 2118.

Vol. 8 page 5.

AUGUST 1916.

Place	Date	Hour	Summary of Events and Information	Remarks and references to Appendices
		9.30 p.m	C.O. ordered O/S C Coy 10th N.F. to send 1 platoon W. along A.C.2. to join up with BLAKE.	
		10.30 p.m.	C.O. sent an orderly to Lt. CLARKE to get point 73 at any cost.	
		10.42 p.m.	Lt. TARGET telephoned that the bombing party was 30 yards from 73 which is full of the enemy blocked with barbed wire and two machine guns firing down our trench.	
		10.59 p.m.	C.O. ordered Capt. BLAKE with his remaining 16 men to move W. to MUNSTER ALLEY between O.G.1 and Point 41.	
		11 p.m.	Lt. CLARKE sent message received 11.30 p.m.:- "My party tried up about 30 yards in front of 73 by barbed wire and a machine gun firing down trench. Have sent party of C. Coy under TARGET up MUNSTER ALLEY to try and get round wall by going over the open. Have no more men to send as a wave."	
		11.10 p.m.	"Got 16 have another try." None message from Bde. Major.	
		11.10 p.m. (Recd. 1.25 a.m 5th)	Received following lookout from Lt. CLARKE:- "Yager's track and reports that not able about 120 yards up MUNSTER ALLEY. There is here a lot of wire and about 50 yards away the trench is full of Boch. He tried to get out the open but was killed at once by M.G. fire. I think we may clear Boch away if Stokes gun comes up in time."	
NEAR CONTALMAISON	5.8.16. 12.5 am		Ordered O/S C Coy 10th N.F. to proceed up GLOSTER ALLEY and relieve Lieut. BUTTERWORTH in BUTTERWORTH TRENCH.	6.
		12.30 am	Ordered Lieut. BUTTERWORTH (E.3. 69) as follows:- "Proceed found the task with your Company and form up there for the attack aaa Your bombard and tools move as quickly as possible." No 2:- Lieut. BUTTERWORTH was prevented from carrying out above from by our own artillery fire.	

WAR DIARY
or
INTELLIGENCE SUMMARY.

Vol. 8   Page 6.   Army Form C. 2118.

AUGUST 1916.

Date	Hour	Summary of Events and Information
5.8.16	1.40 am	Brigadier on advice of Brigade Major decided not to carry out another attack
	1.47 am	Captain LINCOLN O/c B.Coy. 10th N.F. telephoned being heavily shelled by own artillery.
	1.49 am	Lieut BEALE 10th N.F. Bring's phoned he had taken up position in O.G.2. to which he had been ordered by Brigade after it had been evacuated by C.Coy. 10th N.F.
	2.3 am	Lieut DAVENPORT phoned our guns were shelling his platoon on left of BUTTERWORTH TRENCH.
	2.50 am	Lieut CLARKE phoned that TARGET was killed and most of his men; that he was collecting men of D.Coy under 2/Lieut SAINT and ATKINSON and sending them up MUNSTER ALLEY.
	11.55 pm (4.8.16)	Received following message from 68th Inf. Bde.:- "Airforce report your men fighting in TORR TRENCH at 11.25 p.m."
	2.53 am	Sent following message to Lt. BUTTERWORTH at B.Coy.:- "Send a strong bombing party up MUNSTER ALLEY to told our Block" Note:- Owing to our artillery shelling our front line Lt BUTTERWORTH cannot have received this message till after 3.45 am
	3.33 am	Asked Lt. CLARKE to supply 2/Lt BATTY with 10 men to go round to W. entrance to TORR TRENCH and try and get thence morter from ANZACS.
	3.4 am	Received following from LIEUT CLARKE:- "We must have reinforcements up at once as the platoon of A.Coy has not turned up and the men I have got here are being rifle hole with revolvers."
	3.4 am	Gave 2/Lt BATTY message for BUTTERWORTH to reinforce MUNSTER ALLEY with one platoon at once.
	4.9 am	Forward F.O.O. reported that our party in MUNSTER ALLEY was being heavily bombed, but that we were apparently holding our own

7.

WAR DIARY or INTELLIGENCE SUMMARY.

Army Form C. 2118.
Vol. 8 Page 4
August 1916

Place	Date	Hour	Summary of Events and Information	Remarks and references to Appendices
		4.30am	Brigade ordered C/B B. Coy. 10th N.F. (Capt. Ellis) to send strong bombing party of 25 to Munster Alley and relieve A. Coy. Lieut. Butterworth killed.	
		4.45am	A. Coy's bombing party relieved.	
		9am	2/Lt. Rees wounded.	
		7.30pm	Battalion relieved by 8th Yorkshire Regt. Lt.Col. Vaughan commanding and marched to billets in Albert arriving 11.35 P.m. Al-shaw-fhm an enemy shell burst near Col. Vaughan wounding Lieut stunning Major Weston 2nd in Command 8th Yorks and seriously wounding Lieut. Felton the F.O.O. W.N. Davenport 2/Lieut took Command of A. Coy vice Lieut Butterworth killed.	

		8.35pm	The Military Medal Awarded to:-
			No. 17064 Pte W. Luke 23407 Pte W. Simms
			      17809 " J.J. Wilkinson 24496 " W. Vaughan
			      15384 Cpl T. Bellerby
			During the 4th & 10th N.F. snipers accounted for 15 Bock and on the 5th 17.
			Casualties 4.8.16 Capt. R.H.P. Austin missing 2/Lieut N. Thompson wounded (Lieut 5.8.16) 2/Lt W.L. Oakes wounded, 2/Lt E.W. Atkinson wounded at duty. 2/Lieut C.L. Brown wounded at duty. O.R. 6 Killed, 13 wounded, 1 self-inflicted wound, 9 Shell shock, 6 missing
			Casualties 5th:- Lieut E.S. Kaye-Butterworth Killed. Lieut N.R. Target Killed. 2/Lieut F.L.F. Rees wounded. 2/Lieut J.C. Batty wounded at duty. O.R. 4 killed, 18 wounded, 3 shell shock, 5 missing.
				8.

ALBERT	6.8.16		Weather fine. Enemy bombarded Albert all night from 11.30pm to 4am	

Army Form C. 2118.

Vol. 8 Page 8.

WAR DIARY
or
INTELLIGENCE SUMMARY.
(Erase heading not required.)

August 1916.

Place	Date	Hour	Summary of Events and Information	Remarks and references to Appendices
ALBERT	7.8.16	2pm	Battalion marched to bivouac near BECOURT WOOD E. of ALBERT. Battalion H.Q. remained in ALBERT. Casualties:- 18396 B.S.M. W. Brown wounded self-inflicted. Weather fine	9.
	8.8.16	10am	Battalion move to bivouac W. of ALBERT. Enemy shelled ALBERT night of 6/7th. Weather fine.	
LA HOUSSOYE		6am	Enemy shelled ALBERT night of 7/8th. Battalion relieved by 7th Bn. CAMERON HIGHLANDERS (44th Bde. 15th Div.) and marched via MILLENCOURT – LAVIEVILLE BRESLE – FRANVILLERS to billets in LA HOUSSOYE arriving 9-30am. Transport brigaded under Bde. Transport Officer (Lt. A.F.B. HOWARD) Composing 44th Bde:- 8th SEAFORTHS 9th BLACK WATCH 8/10 GORDON HIGHLANDERS 7th CAMERONS 9th GORDON HIGHLANDERS.	

"	9.8.16	7pm	Weather hot. G.O.C. 23rd Div. presented the ribbon of the Military Medal to :-
			No. 15384 Cpl. T. BELLERBY
			      17054 Pte W. LUKE
			      24796 " W. MAUGHAN	

		3pm	C.O.s. Conference at Bde. H.Qrs.	

WAR DIARY or INTELLIGENCE SUMMARY

Army Form C. 2118.

Vol. 8 page 9.

August 1916.

Place	Date	Hour	Summary of Events and Information	Remarks and references to Appendices
LA HOUSSOYE	10.8.16		Rain night 9/10th - Cloudy.	
		3 p.m.	Transport, mounted personnel and Lewis guns moved to POULAINVILLE via QUERRIEU	
VILLERS-SOUS-AILLY	11.8.16		Weather fine - hot.	
		8.20 a.m.	Battalion moved to FLECHINCOURT, arriving 9-10 a.m.; entrained 2 p.m.; and arrived LONGPRÉ 8.45 p.m. marched to VILLERS-SOUS-AILLY arriving 11-40 p.m. Transport proceeded by road arriving 3 p.m.	
"	12.8.16		Weather hot. 2/Lt V.L.D. BERRY joined Battalion.	
CAISTRE	13.8.16		Weather cooler; slight rain night 12/13th	
		12.45 a.m.	Transport marched to LONGPRÉ and entrained	
		3.32 a.m.	Battalion left VILLERS-SOUS-AILLY marched to LONGPRÉ entraining and left 6.41 a.m. via ABBEVILLE, ETAPLES, BOULOGNE, ST OMER, HAZEBROUCK, to BAILLEUL: left BAILLEUL 4-10 p.m. and marched via METEREN and FLÊTRE to CAISTRE arriving 6-40 p.m. Joined 1st Corps area.	
"	14.8.16		Weather fine - windy.	
		9.30 a.m.	H.M. the King and H.R.H. the Prince of Wales rallied at CAISTRE on way through.	
STEENWERCK	15.8.16		Weather dull and cooler. Rain during a.m. 2/Lieut T.R. KELLY arrived.	10.
		2.30 p.m.	Battalion marched to STEENWERCK arriving 7 p.m.	

WAR DIARY or INTELLIGENCE SUMMARY

Army Form C. 2118.

Vol. 8 page 10

August 1916.

Place	Date	Hour	Summary of Events and Information	Remarks and references to Appendices
ARMENTIÈRES	16.8.16	11.45 am	Weather dull. Battalion left STEENWERCK and marched to billets in ARMENTIÈRES (C.25.a.6.9.) arriving 2-45 p.m. Transport at (B.19.b.3.7.) 1 Platoon B. Coy under 2/Lt ATKINSON marched to trenches and relieved garrison at LYS FARM (C.15.d.2.6.) Battalion relieved 20th Durham L.I. 123rd Bde. 41st Div. MAJOR M.E. LINDSAY 7th Dragoon Guards reported his arrival and took command of the Battalion. MAJOR C.E. WALKER returned from hospital. Composition of 1Xth CORPS :- 19th, 23rd & 36th Divisions.	
	17.8.16	9 pm	Weather dull, showers. Battalion left billets at ARMENTIERES, marched to trenches and relieved 23rd MIDDLESEX (Lt.Col. ASH commandg.) relief complete 12-10 a.m. 18th Disposition :- Right Coy. A. Coy. from CARTER'S FARM N.6. trench 92. Coy. 15 supplying post of 1 Officer & 12 men at AILSA CRAIG by night. Left Coy. B. Coy. from trench 93.16 trench 94 patrol GAP C. and with 1 platoon in support at 93.S.1. Support Coy. E. Coy. trenches 93.5.2 - 91.5. Reserve Coy. D. Coy. STATION REDOUBT; held by night 2 command Posts behind GAP C. Battalion H.Qrs. at C.9.D.3.4. Casualties :- Nil.	

Army Form C. 2118.

Vol. 8 Page 11.

WAR DIARY
or
INTELLIGENCE SUMMARY.

(Erase heading not required.)

AUGUST 1916.

12.

Place	Date	Hour	Summary of Events and Information	Remarks and references to Appendices
	18.8.16		Weather wet. Wind W.N.W.	
			Enemy very quiet: night 17/18th and day 18th	
		4 p.m.	G.O.C. 18th Bde 51st Div (Bde at Bois GRENIER) called and had tea.	
			BRIG-GEN. G.N. COLVILLE D.S.O. took command of Bde vice BRIG-GEN. H.P. CROFT.	
			Casualties:- Nil.	
	19.8.16		Weather fine. Wind W.N.W.	
			Enemy very quiet.	
			Casualties:- O.R. 1 wounded	
	20.8.16		Wind W. by N. light weather fine.	
			MAJOR G. WHITE admitted to hospital	
			Enemy quiet	
			Casualties :- Nil	
	21.8.16		Wind W.N.W. light; weather fine.	
			Enemy quiet.	
		7.45 p.m	Captain J.R.L. DOWNEY returned.	
		7.30 p.m	A. Coy relieved by C. Coy and B. Coy by D. Coy.	
		7.45 p.m.	C. Coy returned to AILSA CRAIG.	
	22.8.16		Wind N.W. Light; weather fine	
		2.30 a.m	C/6 D. Coy sent out a patrol from C.10.B.2.4. consisting of	
			No. 17613 CPL. W. PROCTOR	
			24793 PTE. C. SMITH	
			205.19 " C. LANG	

WAR DIARY
or
INTELLIGENCE SUMMARY
(Erase heading not required.)

Army Form C. 2118

Vol. 8 Page 12.

AUGUST 1916.

Instructions regarding War Diaries and Intelligence Summaries are contained in F.S. Regs., Part II. and the Staff Manual respectively. Title Pages will be prepared in manuscript.

13.

Place	Date	Hour	Summary of Events and Information	Remarks and references to Appendices
	23.8.16		Bombing was heard near enemy line at C.4.B.4.½.S. about half an hour later and patrol did not return. Wind S.E. Enemy shelled HIGH COMMAND No.3 and LONG AVENUE and the right of AILSA CRAIG damaging our wire. Casualties :- O.R. 3 missing	
	24.8.16		Wind S.W.	
		6 a.m.	B. Coy moved from STATION REDOUBT and relieved 10th N.F. at trenches 95. 16.½ Coy in 99 with 2½ platoons. One platoon in support at C.U.C.Y.Z. sheet 36.N.W. ½ platoon in 7 TREES REDOUBT.	
		7.30 pm	LONG AVENUE shelled. Casualties :- O.R. 2 wounded, 1 self-inflicted wound.	
	25.8.16		Wind S.E.	
		8.30 am	Relieved by 12th D.L.I. and went into support. Disposition :- Headquarters A. Coy. B. Coy. C. Coy. D. Coy.	C.13.8.1.9. C.9.D.8.6. U.26.C.Y.5. 2 platoons v U.27.a.5.2. 2 platoons C.8.C.8.9. C.8.C.3.Y.
			Casualties :- Nil	
	26.8.16		Wind S.W. Casualties :- Nil	

WAR DIARY or INTELLIGENCE SUMMARY.

Vol. 8 Page 13.
August 1916.

Place	Date	Hour	Summary of Events and Information	Remarks and references to Appendices
	27.8.16		Wind S.W. 2/Lieut. E. GRAY from 20th Hussars reported his arrival. Casualties :- Nil.	
	28.8.16		Wind S.W. ROUMANIA reported to have declared war on AUSTRIA. Casualties :- Nil.	
	29.8.16		Wind S.E. Gas attack and raid by 10th N.F. for tonight was cancelled at 8 p.m. Casualties :- Nil.	
	30.8.16		Wind S.W. Wet and thundery night 29/30th Following Officers reported their arrival from 23rd Batt D.L.I. 2/Lieut S.A. SHARPE 2/Lieut R.S. MITCHELL 2/Lieut S.F. CHAPMAN 2/Lieut A.B. CANDLER.	
		1.30am	Gas was let off from trench 96-104, 113-117 and 121-124 and smoke was interspersed along the front from Le TOUQUET to 124, lasting for 20 minutes. Two Officers and 30 O.R. from 10th N.F. attempted to raid enemy trenches between C.4.a.8½.12. and C.4.c.8½.8. Both Officers were slightly wounded and a few O.R. were casualties. Four men succeeded in entering enemy trench. Casualties :- Nil.	

14.

WAR DIARY or INTELLIGENCE SUMMARY

Army Form C. 2118.

Vol. 8 pages 14

AUGUST 1916.

Place	Date	Hour	Summary of Events and Information	Remarks and references to Appendices
	31.8.16		Wind S.W. The undermentioned officer awarded the Military Cross:- 2/Lt. F.L.F. REES The undermentioned N.C.O. awarded D.C.M. 16194 Sgt. H. CRADDOCK Casualties:- O.R. 1 wounded.	

J.E. Turner Major
COMDG. 13th (SERV.) Bn. DURHAM LT. INFTY.

WAR DIARY or INTELLIGENCE SUMMARY

(Erase heading not required.)

Army Form C. 2118

13th D.L.I. Vol. 9 Page 68
SEPTEMBER 1916.

Place	Date	Hour	Summary of Events and Information	Remarks and references to Appendices
	1.9.16	2.pm	The C.O. Adjt. and 4 Company Commanders of 11th Bn. SHERWOOD FORESTERS called to arrange taking over own billet tomorrow. 2nd inst.	
		3 pm	2/Lt. A. HUDSPETH reported his arrival from 16th Bn. D.L.I.	
		6.45 pm	All moves for tomorrow cancelled. (68th Inf. Bde. wire BM.147.)	
		8.0 pm	Furnished 3 Carrying Parties each of 1. Officer & 42. O.R. for carrying Gas Cylinders out of the trenches.	
	2.9.16	11.9 pm	Received "S.O.S. Gas" and "Stood to" until 11.45 pm, when it was cancelled.	
BAILLEUL	3.9.16	5.30 pm	Relieved by the 7th Bn. Argyll & Sutherland Highlanders. 154th Inf. Bde. 51st Div: and proceeded to a Camp about 1 mile S.E. of BAILLEUL.	
FLETRE	4.9.16		Rain night of 3/4th. Rain this day. Battalion marched to FLETRE at 10.15 am arriving 1 pm.	
NORBECOURT	5.9.16		Weather dull, showers. 12. Noon. Battalion marched to BAILLEUL, entrained and proceeded to ST. OMER. detrained and marched to Billets at NORBECOURT arriving 10.55 pm. Transport except cookers etc by road arriving billets 1 pm. 6th inst.	
	6.9.16		Weather fine.	
	7.9.16	11.30 am	G.O.C. Division (Maj. Genl. Babington) Presented the ribbon of the D.C.M. to No. 16194 L/Sgt. H. CRADDOCK and the ribbon of the Military Medal to No. 12957 Sergt. J. SMITH	
		4 pm	G.O.C. 68th Inf. Bde. inspected the Battalion by Companies.	

Army Form C. 2118.

WAR DIARY
or
INTELLIGENCE SUMMARY.
(Erase heading not required.)

Vol. 9. Page 2.

SEPTEMBER 1916.

Place	Date	Hour	Summary of Events and Information	Remarks and references to Appendices
WARBECOURT	7.9.16		Brigade HQ. moved to CHATEAU COCOVE (RECQUES) 1½ miles N.W. of NORDASQUES. Received following reinforcements 2/Lt. C.H.D. MANN 21st DLI. " F.C. ALLEN 21st DLI. 2/Lt. J.L. BAGGULEY returned to Battalion.	
	8.9.16		Weather fine.	
	9.9.16	9.10 p.m	Weather fine. B. Coy. proceeded to AUDRICQUE as loading party for Brigade.	
	10.9.16		Weather dull.	
		11.30 a.m.	Battalion marched to AUDRICQUE, entrained and arrived LONGEAU at 1 am. 11th inst.	
	11.9.16	1.40 a.m	Weather fine. Battalion left LONGEAU and marched to MOULLIENS-AUX-BOIS arriving 2 p.m.	
		6.55 a.m.	B Coy. (remainder) arriving 2 p.m.	
MILLENCOURT	12.9.16		Weather dull. Battalion moved 6.42 pm to billets and bivouacs at MILLENCOURT in rear of Brigade.	
	13.9.16		Weather showery.	
	14.9.16		Weather fine.	
	15.9.16		Weather fine. Battn standing to from 6.30 a.m.	
		11.30 a.m	Battalion moved to BECOURT WOOD arriving 3.45 pm. Battn under one hours notice to march.	

Army Form C. 2118.

Vol. 9 Page 3.

September 1916

WAR DIARY
or
INTELLIGENCE SUMMARY.
(Erase heading not required.)

Place	Date	Hour	Summary of Events and Information	Remarks and references to Appendices
BECOURT WOOD	16.9.16	1.15 a.m.	Slight rain. Battalion marched via FRICOURT to BAZENTIN-LE-GRAND arriving 5.30 a.m. attached 140th Inf. Bde. 47th Div.	
		10 p.m.	Enemy fired lachrymatory shells on crossroads at BAZENTIN-LE-GRAND and Batt. H.Q. Casualties: 2 O.R. wounded	
BAZENTIN-LE-GRAND	17.9.16		Weather dull. Batt'n furnished carrying and working parties to its full strength for 140th and 141st Inf. Bdes Day and night. 2/Lt V.L.D. BEART & 2/Lt A. HUDSPETH in charge of a bomb-carrying party to 6th LONDON Regt came under an enemy barrage which dispersed his party 2/Lt BEART collected about 45 O.R. and proceeded with his party but was almost at once wounded whereupon Sgt CRADDOCK and Pte FITTS (though ignorant of the route and the guides having disappeared) reconnoitred the way and finally conducted the party to the 6th LONDON REGT. Casualties:- 2/Lt. V.L.D. BEART killed; O.R. 2 killed, 9 wounded.	
"	18.9.16		Weather wet. Furnished 432 O.R. carrying parties Casualties: O.R. 1 wounded	
"	19.9.16		Rain all day.	
		10.30 a.m.	Staff captain 140th Inf. Bde. 47th Div. having reported on previous night that his brigade objectives had all been gained (visited Batt. H.Q. and reported that enemy had counter-attacked during the night and secured possession of the junction of FLERS LINE and DROP ALLEY at M.29 D.5.4. and regained the west of all our bombing sections to regain it: this the C.O. refused but lent him Capt. B.H. CLARKE and his Coy. Blocks had been established in M.29 D.3.3, in O.G.1 at M.29 D.7.3 and in	

Volume 9. Page 4.
Army Form C. 2118

WAR DIARY
or
INTELLIGENCE SUMMARY
(Erase heading not required.)

September 1916.

Place	Date	Hour	Summary of Events and Information	Remarks and references to Appendices
O.G.2.		at about M.29.d.8.3.	At 6.45 pm. after a Stokes Mortar preparation bombing attacks were all three tried & were to be made supported by machine guns, with the object of establishing blocks at about M.29.B.1.2 and M.29.B.2.3 2 Bombing Section 13th D.L.I. under 2/Lt. HUDSPETH attacked up DROP ALLEY 2 bombing sections 13th D.L.I. under 2/Lt. MITCHELL attacked up O.G.1 with the remainder of the Company under Capt. I.H. CLARKE behind them to act as carrying and consolidating parties. Bombing sections of the New Zealand Regt attacked up O.G.2 in conjunction, with the following results:- On Drop Alley the bombing sections advanced some 70 yards before reaching the German block which was heavily wired. The second bombing section fired rifle bombs from and into the enemy over the heads of the first section. The Germans replied very heavily with bombs and counter-attacked over the open, driving the remains of the 2 bombing sections back to our original block which they held till relieved; 2/Lt HUDSPETH and the majority of these two sections were casualties. On O.G.1. the two sections had a sharp bombing fight lasting 10 minutes and then managed to advance some 30 yards up to Drop Alley where they were held up owing to a shortage of bombs and came under bomb fire from 2 directions. The consolidating party made a double block at this point. By this time our artillery had started firing and for over 4 hours shelled the 130 yards we had captured. The block we had made was twice knocked down and finally we had to retire about 20 yards and make a new block which we held until relieved some 6 hours later	
		4.30 pm	The Battalion less B Co. moved via CONTALMAISON to BECOURT WOOD and bivouaced	

WAR DIARY or INTELLIGENCE SUMMARY

Volume 9 Page 5
Army Form C. 2118

September 1916

Place	Date	Hour	Summary of Events and Information	Remarks and references to Appendices
BECOURT WOOD	20.9.16	5 a.m.	Casualties:- 2/Lt. A HUDSPETH missing; O.R. killed 3, wounded 20, missing 7. Weather fine, cold. B Coy relieved and marched to BECOURT WOOD, arriving 11 a.m. Received reinforcement: 2/Lt. P. OWEN 3rd DLI; 2/Lt. J. YOUNG 17th DLI.	
"	21.9.16		Weather fine. Casualties:- O.R. wounded 4.	
"	22.9.16	10:30 a.m. 4:30 p.m.	Weather fine. C.O. attended conference at Bde H.Q. Contalmaison. Battalion moved to support line; disposition:- H.Q. X.12.A.2.6 one O.G.1. One Company BACON TRENCH S.1.B.3.5; 2nd platoon CAMERON TRENCH S.1.D.3.8 to S.1.B.1.1½ and 3 platoons S.1.B.2.1 to S.1.B.3.2; one company S.1D.1.6.6 X.1.A.6.1 HIGHLAND TRENCH and X.1.D.4.4 to S.1.D.0.5 LANCS TRENCH; one company Butterworth Trench X.6.C.5.6 to X.6.C.3.7 and SHETLAND ALLEY to X.6.C.8.7. 2/Lt. H. RUDLAND 20th DLI reported his arrival. Casualties:- O.R. 1 killed, 5 wounded.	
Support trenches X.12.A.2.6	23.9.16		Weather fine, hot. Casualties:- Lt.Col. M.E. LINDSAY wounded at duty; O.R. killed 1, wounded 3.	
"	24.9.16	10:15 p.m.	Weather fine. 2/Lt. GRAY guided 2 tanks to factory line, arriving 2 a.m. Casualties:- O.R. wounded 6.	
"	25.9.16	8 p.m.	Weather fine. D Coy relieved one company 11th N.F. in front line trenches (Martin Alley & Starfish Line; relief complete 10.40 p.m.	

Volume 9. Page 6
Army Form C. 2118

WAR DIARY or INTELLIGENCE SUMMARY

September 1916

Place	Date	Hour	Summary of Events and Information	Remarks and references to Appendices
Support Trench X.12.A.2.6	26.9.16	11:35pm	Enemy shelled Battn H.Q. in O.G.1 with 4.2. Casualties: Capt. J.A.L. DOWNEY wounded at duty, 2/Lt. F.C. ALLAN wounded; O.R. killed 3, wounded 3.	
		4:30am	Battn (less D Co) left O.G.1 and relieved 11th Battn N.F.s (Lt. Col. Caffin comdg) in right battalion sector.	
		10am	Patrols to points 53 and 73 established that enemy held both points and had formed a block in trench below 53.	
		12:30pm	Canadians attacked E of Courcelette.	
		2:55pm	Stokes guns ordered to fire on point 58 succeeded in placing all their shots 100 yds left thereof.	
			Lt. MARKHAM returned from England. Battalion relieved by 11th SHERWOOD FORESTERS 70th Inf. Bde, Lt. Col. WATSON comdg and marched to Bivouac N.E. of BECOURT WOOD. Casualties:- Capt. J.A.L. DOWNEY wounded at duty; O.R. 1 killed, 2 wounded.	
BECOURT WOOD	27.9.16		Weather dull. Enemy shelled MARTINPUICH all day	
BECOURT WOOD	28.9.16		Weather fine wet. Weather wet; rain all day.	
"	29.9.16			
"	30.9.16		Weather fine.	

Eastbourne (a.a.g Adjt)
Lt. Col:
COMDG. 13th (SERV) BN. DURHAM LT. INFTY.

13 D.L.I.

Vol 15

WAR DIARY or INTELLIGENCE SUMMARY
(Erase heading not required.)

Army Form C. 2118
Vol. 10 page 1 68/23
October 1916

Place	Date	Hour	Summary of Events and Information	Remarks and references to Appendices
BECOURT WOOD	1.10.16		Wind S.W. Rain. Battalion resting in bivouacs N.E. of BECOURT WOOD. Transport at M.20.C.	
		10 am	Battalion under 15 minutes notice to move to PEAKE WOOD	
		7 pm	Hostile aircraft dropped bombs on MAMETZ WOOD. Casualties: Nil.	
"	2.10.16		Wind S.W. Rained all day.	
		2.15 pm	Battalion moved to PEAKE WOOD arriving 3.30 pm. Casualties Nil.	
"	3.10.16		Wind S.W. Rain. Battalion relieved 8th Battn DURHAM LIGHT INF, 149th Inf. Bde., 50th Div. — relief complete 11 am. Dispositions:— H.Q. M.33.D.4.6. A & C Coys PRUE TRENCH; D & B Coys STAR FISH LINE. Transport & 2.M. remain at M.20.C. Battalion H.Q. shelled at intermittently all day. Casualties:— Nil.	
MARTINPUICH Trenches M.33.D.4.6	4.10.16		Weather wet. Wind S.W. Casualties: 1 O.R. wounded	
"	5.10.16	5 am	Weather dull. Trenches very muddy. Fatigue party of 50 O.R.s to 10th N.F. returning 10.30 am.	
		2.30 pm	CHAPMAN took 50 boxes bombs to 10th N.F. C.O. attended conference at Bde H.Q.	
		11 pm	47th Div. on our right took "the MILL" at M.22.B.9.6 Casualties:— 2 O.R. wounded O.R.C. Coy under 2/Lt	

Army Form C. 2118

Vol. 10 page 2

October 1916

WAR DIARY or INTELLIGENCE SUMMARY

(Erase heading not required.)

Place	Date	Hour	Summary of Events and Information	Remarks and references to Appendices
MARTINPUICH TRENCHES M.33.D.4.6	6.10.16		Weather fine.	
		6.15pm	Relief of 11th Battn. N.F. (Major Lord LOVELACE Commanding) by the Battalion commenced in front of operations against "the TANGLE", E. of LE SARS.	
		9.15pm	Completion of relief delayed by 11th N.F. operations against "the TANGLE", E. of LE SARS:	
		10pm	11th N.F. attacked the TANGLE; attack failed	
		11.15pm	Relief of 11th N.F. by the Battalion completed. Dispositions:	
			H.Q. in 26A Ave. M.21.D.9.7; B & C Coys in O.9.2 (C. Coy on right); A & D Coys in O.9.1 (A Coy on left)	
			Recd draft of 89 O.R. from 3rd D.L.I. (Reserve Battn.)	
			Casualties:- O.R. 2 killed, 1 wounded.	
LE SARS TRENCHES M.21.D.9.7	7.10.16		Weather dull	
		7.30am	Conference of Coy Commanders at Battn. H.Q.	
			Narrative of operations carried out by 13th D.L.I. at LE SARS on 7.10.16 :-	
			1) Orders were received from 68th Inf. Bde. (6.10.16) that the Battalion would attack and take N.E. portion of LE SARS after the 12th D.L.I. had taken the SUNKEN ROAD on the East of it and bg the Bde of 12th D.L.I. the S.W. portion of it, that when the N.E. portion was in our hands, strong posts were to be established about M.16 A.8.3 to gain touch with the 6q th Inf Bde at M.16 B.0.3 and M.16 B.3.0. In order to keep touch with progress made by 12th D.L.I. in their attack on SUNKEN ROAD, I was instructed to detail an officers Patrol to proceed on left of 12th D.L.I.	
			2) The operations were discussed on 3 separate occasions with all Officers and N.C.Os. who were instructed to go into these details with their men. During to the Battalion being so weak, companies were organised into 2 Battalions the strongest of which was not nearly equal to platoon establishment. Platoons were organised into groups of 6 consisting of 1 N.C.O. 2 bayonet men and 3 bombers. each	

Army Form C. 2118.

Vol 10 page 2

October 1916

WAR DIARY
or
INTELLIGENCE SUMMARY
(Erase heading not required.)

Place	Date	Hour	Summary of Events and Information	Remarks and references to Appendices

bombers carried 12 bombs in their haversacks. The remainder of the men each carried two bombs in their haversacks. The bombers carried rifles slung and 2 bandoliers of ammunition. The First Coy was detailed to attack N.E portion of LE SARS: the second Company detailed to support former Company and if not used up to cover. Fourth Company the northern end of village and send out patrols. 3rd Company was detailed to consolidate and hold strong points; Fourth Company together with all H.Q. details to act as a reserve and to be prepared to take part in either the clearing of LE SARS or consolidation of strong points. Instructions to every Coy were given that only 3 men per Company were to escort prisoners back and what prisoners should happen to be taken in the area of the 12th D.L.I. or 6th Brigade should immediately be handed over to those units. One Company 11th N.F. was attached to the Battalion for carrying purposes. This Company had carried forward to O.C.I before zero hour a large supply of Bombs, S.A.A. other material and water. During operations prisoners brought in were handed over to 11th N.F. to be escorted back. On the previous night a strong working party was sent to 26th Avenue to clean the trench, complete Battalion H.Q. and Regimental Aid Post and make shelters for bodiereis etc.

3) Operations

1.45 pm   a) At Zero hour (1.45 pm) a patrol of 1 officer and 18 O.R. went forward with the first wave of the 12th D.L.I. The Officer and 5 O.R. got as far as some shell holes close to the SUNKEN ROAD and on the left of the TANGLE where they fired on and bombed the enemy holding the SUNKEN ROAD. The remnants of this patrol eventually got into SUNKEN ROAD when "C" Company attacked it from the E.

b) Progress - No information as to progress of the 12th D.L.I. could be obtained until 2.26 p.m. when it was believed the "Salt" had successfully attacked the TANGLE. At the same time information was received from our patrols who were ordered to

Army Form C. 2118.

Vol. 10 page 7

October 1916

WAR DIARY or INTELLIGENCE SUMMARY

(Erase heading not required.)

Place	Date	Hour	Summary of Events and Information	Remarks and references to Appendices
			keep touch with the 6th Bord attack on the S.W. portion of LE SARS, that the 9th YORKS required reinforcements if they were to be successful. I ordered Capt. BLAKE, the O/C. C. Coy to move forward at once, but to enter the village about M.16.c.2.2. and not SUNKEN ROAD as originally arranged. This Company went over in 2 waves. Captain CLARKE in command of B Coy was ordered to proceed with his Coy in immediate support but to keep more to the left and if necessary to work up through Eastern side of LE SARS. Capt. H.F. BLAKE was killed soon after the advance commenced. The leading wave was stopped by machine gun fire when in about M.16.C.2.1. Reinforced by fragments from second wave they engaged the enemy with rifles and bombs from shell holes. "B" Coy arrived a few minutes later and the machine gun team being out of action, both Companies charged that portion of the village and the SUNKEN ROAD, the 9th YORKS on the left gaining their objective about the same time. "C" Coy bombed the dug-outs in the SUNKEN ROAD and worked up East until all Germans either were killed or had surrendered. Capt. D.H. CLARKE finding that Capt. BLAKE had been killed took charge of forward operations and proceeded at once with B Coy through N.E. portion of LE SARS supported closely by 1 platoon of "C" Coy, the other platoon of "C" Coy remained to consolidate and collect prisoners in the SUNKEN ROAD. In the advance through N.E. portion of LE SARS, little opposition was met in the open; the groups dealt with the enemy in their dug-outs effectively. Patrols were at once pushed out in some cases beyond the divisional barrage; patrols were sent but as follow; on the right to the top of the rising ground where a good view of the BUTTE DE WARLENCOURT and the ground about it could be obtained. On the right centre to a trench about M.16.A.7.6; on the left centre to a trench about M.16.A.0.6 and also to	

WAR DIARY

Army Form C. 2118.

Volume 10 Page 5

October 1916

M.15.B.9.1. - Patrols reported at 3.42 p.m. that they could see no signs of the enemy.

(c) **Consolidation**. I then sent forward "A" Company to consolidate the strong points, while the patrols remained out in shell holes and trenches, acting as covering party during the time the Company consolidated. At 7.50 p.m. this Company reported that Strong Points "were established each with a Lewis Gun. Fresh patrols were sent out and the covering patrols withdrawn at this hour. With the exception of those Strong Points" and that in SUNKEN ROAD, the Battalion (according to instructions) were withdrawn back to O.G.2 and 1.

On receipt of information that the ground to the N.E. of LE SARS was clear, I notified the O/C Coy 9th YORKS and asked him to move forward and establish posts in touch with my left. I also notified O/C 12th D.L.I.

(d) **TANKS**. At 3.30 p.m. I received verbal orders over the telephone that the TANK was to move through LE SARS and attack in rear the enemy that were holding up the left of the 69th Brigade. Later in reply to orders sent to him, O/C TANK reported his machine had been hit by an H.E. shell and was out of action.

(e) **ALTERATIONS IN DISPOSITIONS** - At 9.30 p.m. on 7th instant Brigade Major 68th Bde. brought verbal orders that owing to the failure to obtain objectives on our right and left it would be necessary to strengthen the NORTH end of LE SARS. For this purpose 4 Vickers Guns and 1 Coy of the 11th N.F. were placed at disposal of O/C 13th D.L.I. who sent forward 1 Company 13th D.L.I. with 2 Lewis Guns and established "Strong Posts" with 1 Lewis Gun about M.16.A.9.3. The remainder of the Company and 1 Lewis Gun established themselves at NORTH end of LE SARS about M.16.A.9.1. The Vickers Guns were established as follows:- 2 Guns in NORTH end of LE SARS at M.16.A.9.2 and M.16.B.1½.1. one gun in

WAR DIARY

Army Form C. 2118.

Volume 10 Page 6
October 1916.

Place	Date	Hour	Summary of Events and Information	Remarks and references to Appendices
	8.10.16		SUNKEN ROAD about M.16.C.5.1½ and the 4th Gun in O.G.2 about M.21.B.9.2.4. The "Strong Point" in SUNKEN ROAD was reinforced by remainder of "C" Coy. My reserve Company occupied O.G.2.— The Company of 11th N.F. occupied O.G.1.— Assisted by a small party of R.E. and carrying parties from the 15th Division, the men distributions were able to consolidate and ample reserve of Bombs, S.A.A. etc, with them. wounded 1) CAPTURES:– 1 machine Gun; 1 Officer, 150 O.R. prisoners; 1 Off, 30 O.R. left in LE SARS; estimated enemy killed and wounded 130. Casualties:– Capt. H.F.BLAKE killed, 2/Lt. E.W.ATKINSON, Lt. H.R.MARKHAM wounded; 2/Lt. F. GRAY wounded at duty; O.R. killed 11, wounded 39, wounded at duty 1, missing 5, wounded S.I. 1; Weather dull	
LE SARS TRENCHES M.21.D.9.7		5.30 a.m.	Very heavy bombardment on our left. Enemy heavily shelled LE SARS during the 8th with 5.9s. At 4. p.m. on 7th instant all telephone wires had been cut and all communications thereafter had to be maintained by runner. Telephones immediately after the advance had been laid up to the advanced and other Companies. In the case of the forwards Company 3 separate lines were laid at different times, but with the exception of 2 or 3 minutes it was impossible owing to enemy barrage to keep lines in repair. During the afternoon of the 8th a patrol went out to the north east of LE SARS came in contact with the enemy at about M.16.B.7.7	
		8 p.m.	Relief of Battalion by 9th Battn. BLACK WATCH 15th DIV. commenced Casualties: O.R. Killed 4, wounded 10, wound shock shell 1.	

Army Form C. 2118.

WAR DIARY
or
INTELLIGENCE SUMMARY
(Erase heading not required.)

13th Durham Light Infantry

Volume 10 page 87
October 1916

Place	Date	Hour	Summary of Events and Information	Remarks and references to Appendices
LE SARS TRENCHES M.21.D.9.7	9.10.16	4 a.m.	Relief of Battalion by 9th BLACK WATCH complete. Battalion marched off to bivouac in BECOURT WOOD arriving 8 a.m. Weather fine.	
BECOURT WOOD 10.10.16			Weather fine. Battalion resting.	
"	11.10.16	11 a.m.	Bn. Ind. Bde. inspected by Lt. Gen. Sir Wm PULTENEY K.C.B. Comdg IIIrd Corps	
"		2 pm.	Battalion left BECOURT WOOD, entrained at ALBERT 4 p.m., arrived LONGPRE 7 a.m. 11th Weather dull.	
VILLERS-SUR-AILLY	12.10.16	8 a.m.	Battn. marched from LONGPRE to billets at VILLERS-SUR-AILLY arriving 10 a.m. Transport proceeding by road.	17.
"	13.10.16		Weather dull.	
"		2 p.m.	Battalion marched to ST. RICQUIER arriving 4.15 p.m.; billets.	
ST. RICQUIER	14.10.16		Weather dull.	
"	15.10.16		Weather dull; light showers. Battn. entrained at ST. RICQUIER and proceeded via FREVENT, ST. POL and HAZEBROUCK to PROVEN arriving 4.30 pm; marched to WINNEPEG CAMP arriving 8.50 p.m.	
WINNEPEG CAMP H.19.A.2.5	16.10.16		Weather cold - Battn. resting.	
"	17.10.16		Weather wet	
"	18.10.16		Heavy rain night of 17/18th	

Army Form C. 2118.

Volume 10. Page 8

October 1916

WAR DIARY or INTELLIGENCE SUMMARY
(Erase heading not required.)

18.

Place	Date	Hour	Summary of Events and Information	Remarks and references to Appendices
YPRES	19.10.16	6.15 pm	Battn marched to BRANDHOEK level crossing G.12.D.6.9. entrained at 7.15 pm detrained at the ASYLUM YPRES and marched to Infantry Barracks arriving 9 p.m. Transport & L.G. carts by road. Transport took over Transport lines from 25th Battn 7th Australian Bde 2nd Div. at G.24.C.3.9.	
"	20.10.16		Night of 18/19th wet. — Wind W. Weather wet. — Wind W.	
		5.45 pm	Battalion moved to trenches and relieved 12th Batts D.L.I.; Batts on left 1th L. North Lancs, 165th Bde 55th Div; on right 11th N.F. 68th Inf Bde :— Dispositions:— Right front Coy D Co I.18.C.4½.6 — I.17.B.7.3 Left front Coy B Co I.17.B.7.3 — Culvert, patrolling to BELLEWARDE BEK and Posts Support Co A Co, Bn H.Q. ( ) Aid Post at HALFWAY HOUSE. Reserve Coy (ordered by C.O) to reinforce front line and took up a position in LEINSTER TR.	
		9.40 pm	Relief complete 9.40 pm. Casualties Nil.	
Trenches I.18.C.4½.6 - CULVERT	21.10.16		Weather cold; Night of 20/21. Wind S.E. "dangerous" during the night of 20/22, disposition rearranged as follows:— Left subsection : 1 NCO & 6 O.R. at I.16.A.2½.9 MENIN Bombing post about I.18.A.7.6 on either side of Road consisting of 6 O.R. one L.G. at I.18.A.5.6; one officer 12 OR at the CULVERT; remainder of B Coy in I.17 all french with	

Army Form C. 2118.

Volume 10 page 19
October 1916

WAR DIARY
or
INTELLIGENCE SUMMARY
(Erase heading not required.)

Place	Date	Hour	Summary of Events and Information	Remarks and references to Appendices
Trenches I.18 c 4.4.6 - CULVERT	22.10.16		1 Lewis Gun at BURR CROSS ROADS; half C Coy in French I.17.3 and I.17.2 with Lewis Gun at I.17.2. The other half of this Company (one officer and 30 O.R) and 1 Lewis Gun in southern end of LEINSTER STREET as well as one platoon of support Company as temporary garrison in the same French the last mentioned L.G. is placed at about I.17.3.1.1. Casualties: Nil. Weather cold, frost during night 21/22; wind light variable NE & S.E "tomorrow" warmer in evening. Enemy very quiet all day. Casualties: Nil.	19
"	23.10.16	10.45 am	Wind S.E. light; warmer. Growing misty.	
		9.30 pm	Relief of Batts by 10th (S) Batts W. RIDING Regt (Lt. Col. HAINE Comdg) commenced; raining. Casualties: Nil.	
POPERINGHE	24.10.16	1.30 am	Relief complete. Battalion marched to YPRES via MENIN ROAD, entrained at ASYLUM and detrained at POPERINGHE; in billets 3.30 am. Battalion resting. Weather wet	
"	25.10.16		Battalion provided working parties as follows:— 1 Officer & 50 O.R at Div. Baths from 9 am – 12.30 pm 1 Sgt & 20 O.R. at Div. Baths from 3.30 pm to 6 pm	

Army Form C. 2118.

Volume 10 page 10
October 1916

WAR DIARY
or
INTELLIGENCE SUMMARY

(Erase heading not required.)

Place	Date	Hour	Summary of Events and Information	Remarks and references to Appendices
POPERINGHE	26.10.16		Weather wet. Battalion providing working parties.	
"	27.10.16		Weather dull, slight rain.	
		2.30 p.m.	Gen. Sir HERBERT C.O. PLUMER G.C.M.G, K.C.B, Comdg 2nd Army inspected 68th Inf Bde at football ground POPERINGHE; Gen. Birdwood Comdg Australian Div. present. Battalion providing working parties.	
"	28.10.16		Weather wet. Capt. D.E. SCOTT. R.A.M.C. reported his arrival and relieved Capt. G.M. SHAW. R.A.M.C. Battalion providing working parties.	
"	29.10.16		Weather wet. Battalion returned from hospital and assumed command of the Battalion. Major C.E. WALKER	
		10 a.m.	Lt. Col. R. MANNERS Comdg 68th Inf. Bde presented ribbon of MILITARY MEDAL to:- No. 18315 Pte T. JACKSON B Co No. 18150 Pte N. BROWN B Co 17075 " G.E. NEWBY C Co 46042 " C. NICHOL B Co 16491 L/Cpl. C. GOWLAND B Co 17032 " T. HARLE C Co 16431 Pte J.G. GREEN C Co 15932 " R. CONSTANTINE A Co 21046 " T.Y. BOWMAN H.Q. 21618 Sgt. C.A. STIRLING H.Q. 21614 " D. GRAHAM D Co the Bar of the MILITARY MEDAL to 18777 " R. PURVIS B Co No. 17750 Sgt. M. BROUGH A Co 13304 " J. TOMKIN A Co The Bar of the Military Medal awarded on 28.10.16 to No. 19782 Pte C. O'ROURKE B Co could not be presented, recipient on leave and ribbon to No. 16429 Pte J.E. VIPOND B Co - died	20.

Army-Form C. 2118.

VOLUME 10 Page N° 11

OCTOBER 1916

WAR DIARY
or
INTELLIGENCE SUMMARY
(Erase heading not required.)

Place	Date	Hour	Summary of Events and Information	Remarks and references to Appendices
	30.10.16	5.30 pm	Battalion left billets and marched to POPERINGHE SIDING, entrained 7pm; detrained YPRES ASYLUM and marched to HOSPICE arriving 8.45pm. Taking over billets occupied by 8th (S) Battn YORK & LANCS. Regt, 70th Inf/Bde. Weather wet; wind "DANGEROUS". Whole Battalion on working parties.	
HOSPICE YPRES	31.10.16	11 am	Weather fine am; Raining pm. Whole Battalion on working parties.	

Owens Major
COMDG. 13th (SERV.) Bn. DURHAM LT. INFTY.

WAR DIARY
INTELLIGENCE SUMMARY

Army Form C. 2118.

13 DLI Vol. XI page 1.

November 1916

Place	Date	Hour	Summary of Events and Information	Remarks and references to Appendices
YPRES HOSPICE	1.11.16		Weather wet. Whole Battalion on working and carrying parties	
		5.30pm	Enemy shelled YPRES with whizbangs.	
"	2.11.16	Noon	Weather wet.	
		5pm	Battalion moved to front line and relieved 12th DURHAM LIGHT INF. on left Sector, right Brigade:- Dispositions:- Right Coy A Coy from St. Peters Street I.24.1. to I.24.2 inclusive Left Coy C Coy I.24.3 and I.24.4 inclusive Support Coy B Coy Maple Copse and Stafford Trench I.24. A and B. Reserve Coy D Coy Zillebeke Bund I.21. A.9.8 H.Q. Dormy House I.23 A.7.6 Aid Post I.22.B.8.3 Condition of trenches good excepting VANCOUVER ST and BORDER AVE. very bad. Practically no wire. On left 9th YORKS; on right 11th NF3 Casualties:- 1 O.R. wounded.	
Trenches I.21.1 & I.24.4	3.11.16		Weather fine early, wet during p.m.	
		1.55pm	A British Observation Balloon No. 15 Sec. R.F.C. which had broken loose drifted across behind our line. Our A.A. and enemy A.A. guns shelled the balloon which was last seen flying N.N.W. at a great height. 2/Lt BEVAN the only occupant threw out all maps and papers and descended by parachute at ELVERDINGHE. Enemy quiet: Front line Coys busy wiring. Casualties:- 1 O.R. wounded	

Army Form C. 2118.

Vol. XI page 2.
November 1916

WAR DIARY
or
INTELLIGENCE SUMMARY.
(Erase heading not required.)

Instructions regarding War Diaries and Intelligence Summaries are contained in F.S. Regs., Part II. and the Staff Manual respectively. Title pages will be prepared in manuscript.

Place	Date	Hour	Summary of Events and Information	Remarks and references to Appendices
Trenches I.21.I to I.24.4	4.11.16		Weather fine.	
		3-5pm	8th Batt. YORKSHIRE Regt. on our left relieved by 11th Batt. NOTTS & DERBY'S (Northumberland) Regt. on our left. Relieved by 11th Batt. NOTTS & DERBY'S enemy trench mortar activity on our right caused enemy to retaliate heavily with minnies and field guns on CRAB CRAWL, VANCOUVER ST. and SANCTUARY WOOD. Front line boys busy wiring. Casualties: 1 O.R. killed, two wounded.	
"	5.11.16		Weather fine. Wind dangerous. Enemy shelled YPRES - POPERINGHE road. Front line companies wiring and repairing MINNIE damage	
"	6.11.16		Weather fine. Wind dangerous. Enemy active with M.G's during night of 5/6th. Casualties:- 1 D.R. killed, 1 wounded.	
		7.30pm	Batt. relieved by 12th Durham Light Infy. and marched to "C" Batt's position at the BUND. Dugouts constantly caving in.	
ZILLEBEKE BUND	7.11.16		Rain all day. Wind safe. Battalion on working parties all night. Casualties; Nil	
"	8.11.16		Showers all day; dugouts constantly caving in; working parties all night. Casualties; Nil.	
"	9.11.16		Weather fine. Battalion on working parties; wind safe. Casualties Nil.	
"	10.11.16		Weather fine. Wind safe.	
		8pm	Batt'n relieved by 10th W. Riding Regt. 69th Bde and marched to YPRES; entrained and detrained at VLAMERDINGHE and marched to WINNIPEG CAMP arriving 10pm. Casualties; Nil.	
WINNIPEG CAMP	11.11.16		Weather fine. Warmer. Wind safe.	

Army Form C. 2118.

Vol. XI. page 3.
November 1916

WAR DIARY
or
INTELLIGENCE SUMMARY.
(Erase heading not required.)

Instructions regarding War Diaries and Intelligence Summaries are contained in F.S. Regs. Part II. and the Staff Manual respectively. Title pages will be prepared in manuscript.

Place	Date	Hour	Summary of Events and Information	Remarks and references to Appendices
WINNIPEG CAMP	12.11.16	7.30am	Weather fine. Batts. furnished working party of 50 O.R. B Coy to report to Lt HUSBAND R.E, Officer I/ch. DRAINAGE at DICKEBUSCH BECK H.17.C.7.3.	
		9 pm	Received reinforcement of 70 O.R. from 2nd, 5, 6, 7, 8, & 23rd D.L.I. Casualties Nil.	
"	13.11.16		Fine warm sunshine	
"	14.11.16		Weather fine	
"	15.11.16		Weather cold: E. Wind: frosty night of 14th/15th.	
"	16.11.16		Weather colder: frosty night of 15/16th. Wind E.	
		4.0 pm	Batts. left WINNIPEG CAMP heading over to 8th YORK & LANCS REGT and marched to VLAMERTINGHE; entrained, detrained at ASYLUM YPRES and marched to trenches relieving 8th K.O.Y.L.I. (Lt.Col. IMBERT-TERRY Comdg) in Lt.Batt. Left Bde: relief complete 8.20 pm.	
			Dispositions:— D Coy right Coy I.18.4 and I.18.6 (3 Platoons) with 2 L.Gs and listening post at N.W. corner of ZOUAVE WOOD: 1 Platoon and 1 L.G. in support in ROSSLYN STREET B Co centre Coy 1 Platoon I.17.1 and I.17.2. C. Co. Left Coy 1 N.CO & 6 O.R. at I.18.A.2½.9. bombing post about I.18.A.7.6 on either side of road consisting of 6 O.R: 1 L.G. at I.18.A.5.6 and one in E.REGENT ST. One Officer and 30 O.R. at the culvert remainder of Coy in I.17.4 with one L.G. at BURR CROSSROADS. On support 3 Platoons B Co, with 2 L.Gs in LEINSTER ST. one L.G. which is forward advisors. Reserve Coy Batt: H.Q. and AID POST in HALF WAY HOUSE. Batts. on left 1/4th L. NORTH LANCS 55th Div. Batts. on right 11th N.F.s Casualties Nil.	
TRENCHES I.18.4 to I.17.4	17.11.16		Wind E.S.E. — night of 16/17th bitterly cold.	

Army Form C. 2118
Vol. XI. page 4.
November 1916.

WAR DIARY
or
INTELLIGENCE SUMMARY
(Erase heading not required.)

Place	Date	Hour	Summary of Events and Information	Remarks and references to Appendices
Trenches I.18.d–I.17.d	18.11.16	11 p.m.	Two Russians escaped from enemy lines opposite I.17.2 during early morning. 55th Div. on left raid enemy trenches.	
		5.15pm	1 Platoon D Coy in ROSSLYN ST. moved up and joined remainder of Coy in front line. 1 Platoon B Coy in LEINSTER ST. took over ROSSLYN ST. Casualties: Nil.	
	19.11.16		Weather cold am; wind changing pm; sleet in evening. Enemy quiet.	
	20.11.16		2/Lt. G.R. HESELTON 3rd Bn. D.L.I. reported his arrival and was posted to C.Coy. 6th Kings Liverpools relieved 1/4th L. NORTH LANCS on our left. Weather warmer, wind S.W.; rain most of day. Casualties Nil. Weather dull. Wind S.W.	
		9 pm	12th D.L.I. relieved battalion in trenches; after relief Battalion proceeded to Infantry Barracks Ypres.	
		2.45pm	Enemy shelled Battalion H.Q. with whizbangs. Casualties: Nil	
BARRACKS YPRES.	21.11.16		Weather cold; wind dangerous. Whole Battalion on working parties. Casualties: 1 O.R. wounded. Weather warmer; wind safe.	
"	22.11.16		Whole Battalion on working parties. Casualties: Nil	
"	23.11.16		Weather warm, wind safe.	

Army Form C. 2118.

WAR DIARY
or
INTELLIGENCE SUMMARY
(Erase heading not required.)

Vol XI. page 5
November 1916.

Place	Date	Hour	Summary of Events and Information	Remarks and references to Appendices
BARRACKS YPRES	24.11.16		Battalion on working and carrying parties. Casualties: 1 O.R. wounded.	
		5.30 p.m.	Weather warm; light rain. Wind safe. Batt. left Barracks and relieved 12th D.L.I. in left Batt. left Sector:- Disposition:- A Co. 3 Platoons and 2 L.Gs. I.18.4 and I.18.6 and one platoon and one L.G. in ROSSLYN ST. B Co. with 2 L.G at I.17.3 & I.17.4 and one officer and 20 O.R. with one L.G. at the CULVERT. D Co. one platoon I.17.1 and I.17.2 and 3 Platoons and 2 L.Gs in LEINSTER ST. C. Co. with 3 L.Gs, Batt's H.Q. and First Aid Post at HALF WAY HOUSE Batt's on right: 11th Batt'n N.F., Batt's on left 6th Kings Liverpool Regt. 55th Div. Relief complete 9 p.m. Casualties: Nil.	
TRENCHES I.18.4–I.17.4	25.11.16	10 a.m.	Weather mild, raining. Wind safe. Enemy put 6 whizbangs on left of CULVERT. Casualties Nil.	
	do	10.45 am 12.15 pm	Weather fine; observation good. Wind 6 N.W. Enemy shelled Battalion H.Q. with L.H.V. gun and again at 12.20 pm Working party of 12th D.L.I. on CHINA WALL near GORDON HOUSE shelled by enemy.	

Army Form C. 2118.

Vol. XI page 6
November 1916

WAR DIARY
or
INTELLIGENCE SUMMARY

(Erase heading not required.)

Place	Date	Hour	Summary of Events and Information	Remarks and references to Appendices
		12:45 pm	Enemy shelled road between HELLFIRE CORNER and R.E. DUMP with shrapnel and H.E.	
		3.30 p.m.	Enemy breached CHINA WALL near GORDON DUMP; repaired at night. Casualties nil.	
TRENCHES I.18.4–I.17.4	27/11/16	10 a.m.	Weather fine 8am. clouding over; wind veering to N; colder. Enemy shelled CHINA WALL near GORDON HOUSE with 5.9s	
		9 p.m.	Casualties :- 1 O.R. wounded.	
	28/11/16		Weather cold, very misty all day. Wind slight, N.	
		11 a.m.	Enemy shelled GORDON HOUSE and CHINA WALL with 5.9s. Two Poles belonging 35th Ld. Regt. escaped from FORESTER LANE and came into our lines, out at CULVERT the other at I.18.4.	
		5 p.m.	Casualties: 1 O.R. wounded.	
	29/11/16		Very misty; cold; scarcely any wind.	
		3 a.m.	Patrol proceeded from FORESTER TO CULVERT CULVERT to FORESTER LANE; enemy had large working with covering party out.	
		3:45 p.m.	Heavy bombardment of enemy trenches on our left.	
		4.50 pm	Raiding party from 5th KING'S LIVERPOOLS entered German trenches on our left and took 36 prisoners	
		4.30 pm	Received message from 68th Inf Bde that the two escaped Poles had given information that enemy intended to raid over trenches. 1 L.G. from Reserve Coy ordered up to reinforce Company at the CULVERT. Casualties: Nil	
WINNIPEG CAMP	30/11/16		Battalion relieved by 10th W.RIDINGS (Lt.Col. R.R.RAYMER (S.Staffs Comdg) and marched to YPRES; entrained, detrained at VLAMERDINGHE and marched to WINNIPEG CAMP. Weather cold	

R.R.Raymer
Lt. Col.
COMDG. 13th (SERV.) Bn. DURHAM LT. INFTY.

WAR DIARY or INTELLIGENCE SUMMARY

(Erase heading not required.)

Army Form C. 2118

Vol XII DECEMBER 1916 PAGE 1.

13th Durham L.I. Vol 17

Place	Date	Hour	Summary of Events and Information	Remarks and references to Appendices
WINNIPEG CAMP	1.12.16		Weather still cold. General Babington and Major G. Hawes D.A.Q.M.G. 23rd Division called. Artillery active.	
"	2.12.16	Midnight	Weather slightly warmer. 41st Division did a raid on right of the Division	
"	3.12.16	Midnight	Weather cold. No. 25130 Pte R. Wilson D.Coy run over by lorry and killed.	
"	4.12.16		Weather cold. Wind S.S.W.	
"	5.12.16		Weather slightly warmer; heavy rain night of 4/5th.	
"	6.12.16		Weather mild; rain	
"	7.12.16	4.30pm 9.30pm	Weather mild. Battalion left WINNIPEG CAMP and marched to VLAMERTINGHE; detail at ASYLUM and marched to BUND relieving 11th SHERWOOD FORESTERS. Relief complete. Relieved at WINNIPEG CAMP by 8th YORK & LANCS. REGT. 70th Brigade. Casualties: Nil	
THE BUND	8.12.16		Weather dull. Wind "says" S.W. Battalion found 2 Officers and 215 o.r. for working parties night of 8/9th Casualties: Nil	

Army Form C. 2118.

PAGE 2.

WAR DIARY
or
INTELLIGENCE-SUMMARY.
(Erase heading not required.)

VOL XII

Place	Date	Hour	Summary of Events and Information	Remarks and references to Appendices
THE BUND	9.12.16		Weather dull. Wind S. to S.W. Safe. Battalion found 2 Officers and 215 O.R. for working parties right of 9/10th. Casualties: Nil.	
– " –	10.12.16		Weather dull; rain. Wind S.E. Battalion found 3 Officers and 220 men for working parties right of 10/11th. Casualties: Nil	
– " –	11.12.16		Weather fine a.m. dull p.m.	
		4.15pm	Battalion left the Bund & handing over to 10th N.F. (Major ASHTON comdg) and proceeded to front line relieving 12th D.L.I. (Major PEASE comdg). Relief complete 6.35 pm. Dispositions:– A. Coy. right front Coy. I.24.1. and I.24.2. C. Coy. left front Coy. I.24.3. and I.24.4. B. Coy. close support Coy. WINNIPEG St and REDAN D. Coy. reserve Coy. MAPLE COPSE Batt. H.Q. DORMY HOUSE ; M.T. room ZILLEBEKE St. Battalion on left 9th YORKS 69th Bde; Battalion on right 11th N.F.s Casualties: Nil	
– " –	12.12.16		Weather windy; dull all day; wind S.W. – S.E. Enemy quiet. During night 12/13th 2/Lt. HESELTON claimed to have shot a German officer CROSS St. Lt. Col. M.E. LINDSAY went to hospital. Casualties: Nil.	

WAR DIARY or INTELLIGENCE SUMMARY

Army Form C. 2118.

Vol. XII   Page 3

Place	Date	Hour	Summary of Events and Information	Remarks and references to Appendices
	13.12.16		Weather warmer; fine a.m. Wind S.E. 2/Lt. H.C. BUCKELL 9th Dragoon Guards reported his arrival and posted to A.Coy. Enemy active with T.M.s, 4.2s. and 5.9.s. in a.m. and p.m.	
		4 p.m.	Scheme 4 put into operation. Enemy minnie smashed all wires in ZILLEBEKE St. and damaged CRAB CRAWL in two places. Casualty: Wounded 1 O.R.	
	14.12.16		Enemy active a.m. and p.m. with trench mortars and minnies.	
		10 p.m.	Big Stafé on HILL 60. Casualties: Killed accidentally No. 43423 Pte L.W. PRINCE C. Coy. Wounded 2 O.R.	
	15.12.16		Rain during night of 14/15th. Tactical operation of support and reserve companies on night of 14/15th. Enemy retaliated throat line and supports of Battalion on right and damaged WINNIPEG 67 and 11th N.F. Trenches.	
		4 p.m–4.45 p.m	Enemy heavily bombarded right battalion area, YPRES and duckboards leading to front line. 11th N.F. sent up S.O.S. 40 of the enemy attacked and wounded a sap and dugout leaving 3 killed behind. Casualties: Wounded 3 O.R. 40th Infantry Brigade relieved 69th Infantry Brigade on left 11th SHERWOODS on our left.	
	16.12.16		Weather cold, damp. Enemy quiet; our S.O.S. bombardment damaged enemy trenches considerably.	
		8.20 p.m.	Battalion relieved by 12th D.L.I. (Major Lyndall comdg) and marched to HOSPICE. Casualties: Nil.	

Army Form C. 2118.

WAR DIARY
or
INTELLIGENCE SUMMARY.

(Erase heading not required.)

VOL. XII PAGE 4

Instructions regarding War Diaries and Intelligence Summaries are contained in F.S. Regs., Part II. and the Staff Manual respectively. Title pages will be prepared in manuscript.

Place	Date	Hour	Summary of Events and Information	Remarks and references to Appendices
HOSPICE, 1/PPCLI	17.12.16		Weather cold and damp. Battalion on working parties on night of 17/18.	
" "	18.12.16		Weather cold and damp. Major WALKER returned from leave and assumed temporary command of battalion.	
" "	19.12.16		Weather cold and frosty. The following Officers reported their arrival and were posted to the following Companies:- 2/Lt. C.H. ROLLSTON — B.Coy 2/Lt. G.N. WOOD — A.Coy 2/Lt. F.H.C.D. SMITH — B.Coy 2/Lt. T.L. WITHERSPOON — B.Coy 2/Lt. T. MURGATROYD — C.Coy 2/Lt. J. BRADY — D.Coy 2/Lt. H.B. WATSON — D.Coy	
" "	20.12.16	4 p.m. 8 p.m.	Very cold and frosty. Brigade Major phoned and held back relief for half an hour. Battalion relieved the 12th Bn. L.F. in "B" positition. Disposition:- Batts. H.Qrs. DORMY HOUSE A.Coy. 3 platoons WINNIPEG STREET A.Coy. 1 platoon THE REDAN B.Coy. 3 platoons Junction of CROSS ST. and VANCOUVER to CRAB CRAWL B.Coy. 1 platoon SIXTY STREET. C.Coy. 4 platoons CROSS STREET D.Coy. 4 platoons CRAB CRAWL to ST PETERS STREET. Casualties Nil.	

Army Form C. 2118.

WAR DIARY
or
INTELLIGENCE SUMMARY.
(Erase heading not required.)

VOL. XII PAGE 5.

Place	Date	Hour	Summary of Events and Information	Remarks and references to Appendices
	21.12.16		Weather dull	
		10.20am–11.30am	Enemy fired 20 whizzbangs on to ZILLEBEKE ROAD	
		9.30pm	DORMY HOUSE shelled. Remainder of night quiet. Casualties: Nil	
	22.12.16		Wind S.W. rained during day but a clear night.	
		4.30pm	Enemy shelled ZILLEBEKE and DORMY HOUSE	
		6.0pm	49th DIVISION did a raid at I.29.d.1.4. Enemy retaliated on our right Coy and also blew in LONETREE SAP. Casualties: Killed 3 O.R. Wounded 4 O.R.	
	23.12.16	5.25am	The Division on our left did a raid at C.29.d. Weather windy and wet.	
		9.15pm	The Battalion was relieved by the 8th YORKSHIRE REGT (Lt.Col WESTON comdg.) Arrived in huts at WINNIPEG CAMP taking over from 10th WEST RIDINGS	
WINNIPEG CAMP	24.12.16	1.30am		
— " —	25.12.16		The G.O.C. Division and Brigadier called in the morning. Casualties: Nil	
— " —	26.12.16		Weather fine. Casualties: Nil	
— " —	27.12.16		Very cold and frosty and foggy in the evening. Casualties: Nil	
— " —	28.12.16		Weather calm. The Cinema gave a benefit night to the 13th D.L.I. raising 160 Francs. Casualties: Nil	

WAR DIARY
or
INTELLIGENCE SUMMARY
(Erase heading not required.)

Army Form C. 2118

Vol XII Page 6.

Place	Date	Hour	Summary of Events and Information	Remarks and references to Appendices
WINNIPEG CAMP	29.12.16		Weather. Very wet. Casualties: Nil	
" —	30.12.16		Weather raining in the morning but clear at night. Brigade Boxing competition and 12th D.L.I. Benefit night at Cinema. Casualties: Nil	
" —	31.12.16		Weather: fine	
		6.42 pm	Left YLAMERTINGHE and relieved the 11th SHERWOOD FORESTERS in the BARRACKS. Two Platoons of B. Coy and two Lewis guns in FORTS Nos. 1 and 2 about I.15.d.9.8. Relief complete 8.40 pm. Casualties: Nil.	

Russell Major
Comdg. 13th (SERV.) Bn. DURHAM LT. INFTY

Army Form C. 2118.

WAR DIARY
or
INTELLIGENCE SUMMARY.
(Erase heading not required.)

13 D L I/8
JANUARY 1917 VOL.I. PAGE I.

Place	Date	Hour	Summary of Events and Information	Remarks and references to Appendices
THE BARRACKS YPRES	1.1.17		Weather: Fine. Capt. E. Borrow returned from leave and proceeded to take over as Divisional Commandant at STEENVOORDE.	
		5.30–5.50 p.m	Enemy fired a large number of shells into YPRES between 1 and 2 p.m. Our artillery bombarded the CROSS Rds. at I.6.C. Casualties: 1 O.R. wounded.	
	2.1.17		Weather: Fine. Found working parties of 120 O.R. Following decorations sent in new years honours:— Major Gen. J.M. Babington to be K.C.M.G. Lt. Col. Lord R.H.O. Manners to be C.M.G. Lt. Col. M.E. Lindsay given the D.S.O. Casualties: Nil	
	3.1.17		Weather: Fine. The usual working parties were provided. YPRES was shelled during the day. Capt. G.M. Shaw R.A.M.C. and R.S.M. R. Richardson received Military Cross. Casualties: Nil	
	4.1.17		Weather: Very fine. Relieved the 12th D.L.I. (Lt. Col. MacGregor Comdg.) in B. position.	

Army Form C. 2118.

WAR DIARY
or
INTELLIGENCE SUMMARY.
(Erase heading not required.)

JANUARY 1917.

VOL. 1.   PAGE 2.

Place	Date	Hour	Summary of Events and Information	Remarks and references to Appendices
			Dispositions:	
			A. Coy. I.18.4. to I.17.1. inclusive	
			C. Coy. I.17.3 and 4 and THE CULVERT.	
			D. Coy. 3 Platoons LEINSTER STREET	
			1 Platoon ROSSLYN STREET	
			B. Coy. 3 Platoons HALFWAY HOUSE	
			1 Platoon I.17.2 and EAST REGENT STREET.	
			BATT^N H.QRS. HALFWAY HOUSE	
	5.1.17	8.15pm	Relief complete.	
			Very quiet night. Casualties: Nil.	
			Weather: Very fine	
			A great deal of aircraft activity	
		11 am	GORDON HOUSE shelled	
		1.15pm	4 Whizzbangs fell on HALFWAY HOUSE.	
		2.30-3.35pm	Our artillery bombarded the enemy trenches about the area I.35.a.	
		2.45-4.15pm	A second bombardment took place on enemy front line and support line at I.29.d. and I.35. b.	
			Enemy shelled YPRES all day and caused a large number of casualties to the 69th Infantry Brigade.	
			Casualties: 1 O.R. wounded.	
	6.1.17		Weather: Wind "dangerous". Fine all morning but rain clearing the remainder of the day.	

Army Form C. 2118.

WAR DIARY
or
INTELLIGENCE SUMMARY.
(Erase heading not required.)

JANUARY 1917.

VOL. 1. PAGE 3.

Place	Date	Hour	Summary of Events and Information	Remarks and references to Appendices
	7.1.17		Enemy very quiet. Capt Gray relieved from leave. YPRES heavily shelled in the evening. Casualties: Nil. Weather: Very fine. Great aircraft activity.	
		11.45am	An enemy aeroplane attacked one of ours just behind HALFWAY HOUSE, by swooping down on it. At the same time one of our planes swept down on the enemy and drove it off.	
		12.15am	Enemy lit one of our aeroplanes with anti-aircraft fire and brought it down in flames. The remainder of the day was very quiet. Casualties: Nil. Weather: Fair.	
	8.1.17		A good deal of artillery activity from 9.30 am. THE CULVERT and I.17.4 and I.17.3 were shelled and also LEINSTER ST. Enemy fired about 200 5.9.3 and 4.2.5. in 6" GORDON HOUSE.	
		4.15 pm / 4.45 pm		
		5.45 pm	Relieved by the 12th D.L.I. (Lt Col. MacGREGOR Comdg)	
		10 pm	Battalion arrived in the INFANTRY BARRACKS in "D" Position.	
	9.1.17		Weather: Fair. Usual working parties found.	
		3 pm	Enemy shelled YPRES.	

Army Form C. 2118.

WAR DIARY
or
INTELLIGENCE SUMMARY.
(Erase heading not required.)

JANUARY 1917

VOL I. PAGE 4

Place	Date	Hour	Summary of Events and Information	Remarks and references to Appendices
			Four new Officers arrived & were posted to the following Companies:	
			2/Lt. E. DAVIS A. Coy.	
			Lt. H.B. HOLDSWORTH C. Coy.	
			Lt. H. STEWART C. Coy.	
			Lt. H.W. PRYSE D. Coy.	
	10.1.17		Casualties: 1 O.R. wounded	
			Weather: Wet	
		2.30pm	The Brigadier inspected the drafts.	
			Heavy artillery all day.	
		5.15pm	55th Division raided the enemy's trenches at T.12.a.2.8.	
			Casualties: Nil	
	11.1.17		Weather: Snowing most of the day.	
			Casualties: Nil	
			Weather: Wet	
	12.1.17		Relieved the 12th D.L.I. in B. position	
			Relief complete	
		8.10pm	Dispositions:	
			H.Qrs. HALFWAY HOUSE	
			D. Coy RIGHT Coy	
			B. Coy LEFT Coy	
			C. Coy 3 Platoons LEINSTER STREET	
			1 Platoon ROSSLYN STREET	
			A. Coy 3 Platoons HALFWAY HOUSE	
			1 Platoon I.17.2 and E. REGENT STREET.	

Army Form C. 2118.

WAR DIARY
or
INTELLIGENCE SUMMARY.
(Erase heading not required.)

JANUARY 1917   VOL 1   PAGE 5

Place	Date	Hour	Summary of Events and Information	Remarks and references to Appendices
	13.1.17	9.10pm	S.O.S. went up on our left, and there was a very heavy bombardment for half an hour. The remainder of the night was very quiet. Casualties: Nil Weather: Snowed hard in the morning and dull all day Enemy artillery very inactive all day. Casualties: Nil	
	14.1.17		Weather: Thick fog. A great deal of work was done salving and on the wire in front and behind under cover of the fog. 2/Lt F. HALL and Sgt. H. CRADDOCK made a useful reconnaissance in to FORESTER LANE but found no signs of the enemy. The day was very quiet. Casualties: Nil	
	15.1.17		Weather: Fine; snow in evening. Had the fog been as bad as on the 14th it was intended to send out an offensive patrol with 2 Lewis guns to kill any enemy working parties seen. Very quiet all day. The C.O. and Intelligence Officer of the 9th Yorks came up to take over. Casualties: Nil Weather: Fine.	
	16.1.17	7.30am	Our Lewis Gunners shelled Hill 60 and enemy retaliated at 10-15 am on CR? GR? N? 66 & Pier Battery. Continued firing all day on Hill 60.	

2353 Wt. W2311/1454 700,500 5/15 D. D. & L. A.D.S.S./Forms/C. 2118.

Army Form C. 2118.

WAR DIARY
or
INTELLIGENCE SUMMARY.
(Erase heading not required.)

JANUARY 1917

VOL 1. PAGE 6.

Place	Date	Hour	Summary of Events and Information	Remarks and references to Appendices
	16.1.17	9.50 p.m.	The Battalion was relieved by the 9th YORKSHIRE REGT (Major CLARK comdg). YPRES Railway Station was shelled damaging the rails and causing the Battalion to march to WINNIPEG CAMP arriving there at 2 a.m. 17.1.17. 2/Lt. M. MILLAR & 2/Lt. HAMILTON reported their arrival. Casualties: Nil	
WINNIPEG CAMP	17.1.17	2.30 p.m.	Weather: Snow fell heavily. A lecture was given on Censorship at the Cinema. Casualties: Nil	
" "	18.1.17		Weather: Rained most of day. Went working parties. Casualties: Nil	
" "	19.1.17	12. noon	Weather: Snow & rain all day. A lecture was given at POPERINGHE on "Barrages". The Corps Commander SIR J.L.N. MORLAND K.C.B, K.C.M.G, D.S.O called. Casualties: Nil	
" "	20.1.17		Weather: Very cold and snowing. Casualties: Nil	
" "	21.1.17	11 a.m.	Weather: Frosty. The C.O. and Major DOWNEY M.C. the General with reference to scheme of communication between Infantry and aeroplanes. Casualties: Nil	

Army Form C. 2118.

WAR DIARY
or
INTELLIGENCE SUMMARY.
(Erase heading not required.)

JANUARY 1917   VOL. I.   PAGE 7.

Place	Date	Hour	Summary of Events and Information	Remarks and references to Appendices
WINNIPEG CAMP	22.1.17		Weather: Very cold.	
		9.30am	The Battalion paraded and carried out manoeuvres in conjunction with aeroplanes returning to camp at 12.30 p.m.	
		3 pm	MAJOR GEN. J.M. BABINGTON called.	
			Casualties: Nil	
"	23.1.17		Weather: Very cold	
		3 pm	Conference of Adjutants at Batt. H.Q.	
			8th Yk. & L.I. did a raid about CRAB CRAWL	
			2/Lt. O.J. WILLIAMS reported his arrival & was posted to B. Coy.	
"	24.1.17		Weather: Very cold	
		6.10pm	The Battalion left WINNIPEG CAMP and relieved the 11th SHERWOOD FORESTERS (Lt. Col. Walton comdg) in the BUND.	
		11.30pm	Relief complete	
			Disposition:	
			H.Q., A, B & C. Coys. BUND	
			D. Coy. STAFFORD S^t	
			Casualties: Nil	
	25.1.17		Weather: Very cold	
		12 noon	Enemy put a few shells into N. end of BUND.	
		8 pm	Our trenches had a shoot on J.19.d.	
		8.45pm	Stromboo horn Lend	
			Received wire from Brigade "Reported gas attack against Bolo road	

Army Form C. 2118.

WAR DIARY
or
INTELLIGENCE SUMMARY.
(Erase heading not required.)

JANUARY 1917   VOL 1   PAGE 8

Place	Date	Hour	Summary of Events and Information	Remarks and references to Appendices
of MENIN ROAD	26.1.17		Casualties: 1 O.R. Wounded. Weather: Very cold. Aircraft very active all day. Casualties: Nil.	
	27.1.17	12 noon	Weather: Very cold. G.O.C. Brigade held a conference at our H.Qrs. at the BUND with the Cos. PRATT D.S.O. and Lt Col C.E. WALKER	
		12 noon to 1.30 p.m	The 49th Division bombarded the enemy. Casualties: 1 O.R. wounded	
	28.1.17		Weather: Very cold. Enemy shelled N. end of BUND. The Battalion relieved the 12th D.L.I. in the front line. Dispositions: H.Qrs. RUDKIN HOUSE. A. Coy. I.30.b, 2 and 3 C. Coy. I.30.a, 5 and 6 B. Coy. I.30.7, 8 and 9. D. Coy. HALIFAX STREET	
		8.30 p.m	Relief complete. Capt H.S. OLDHAM relinquishes his commission on account of ill health. Casualties: Nil.	

Army Form C. 2118.

WAR DIARY
or
INTELLIGENCE SUMMARY.
(Erase heading not required.)

JANUARY 1917   VOL. 1.   PAGE 9.

Place	Date	Hour	Summary of Events and Information	Remarks and references to Appendices
	29.1.17		Weather: Very cold. Very quiet all day with the exception of a few shells falling into RODKIN HOUSE. Casualties: Wounded O.R. 1.	
	30.1.17	9.9.30am	Weather: Very cold. Our Heavies bombarded enemy communication trenches & support line in I.19. I.25. and I.30. Casualties: Wounded accidentally O.R. 1. Wounded O.R. 1.	
	31.1.17	11.15am	Weather cold. Enemy shelled our front line at I.30.6. Casualties: Wounded at duty Capt. E. GRAY. Killed O.R. 2. Wounded O.R. 3. Major J.A.L. DONNEY went on leave.	

C. Owen
LT. COL=
13th (SERV.) Bn. DURHAM LT. INFTY.

Army Form C. 2118.

13 DLI
Vol 2. Page 1
February 1917.
Vol 19

WAR DIARY
or
INTELLIGENCE SUMMARY
(Erase heading not required.)

Place	Date	Hour	Summary of Events and Information	Remarks and references to Appendices
	1.2.17	5 a.m.	Weather: Very cold. Enemy opened a very heavy bombardment and the S.O.S. was sent up by the Battalion N. of Menin Rd. Remainder of the day was fairly quiet. Relieved by the 12th Bn D.L.I. and proceeded to "B" position. Dispositions: H.Qrs., C & D Coys. — Bund / A Coy — Riding School / B Coy — Kruisstraat. Casualties: Nil	
	2.2.17		Weather: Very cold. Found working parties of 70 o.r. Casualties: Nil	
	3.2.17		Weather: Very cold. Very quiet all day. Casualties: Nil	
	4.2.17	3-4 pm	Weather: Very cold. Our artillery opened a heavy bombardment at 3pm which lasted until 4pm. Remainder of day very quiet. Casualties: Nil	

Army Form C. 2118.

WAR DIARY
or
INTELLIGENCE SUMMARY   Vol 2.   Page 2.
(Erase heading not required.)

FEBRUARY 1917.

Place	Date	Hour	Summary of Events and Information	Remarks and references to Appendices
	5.2.17		Weather: Very cold	
		5.30pm	Battalion moved up to relieve 12th D.L.I. in "A" position.	
			Disposition:	
			H.Qrs. RUDKIN HOUSE	
			A.Coy. HALIFAX St.	
			B.Coy. I.30.y, 8 & 9	
			C.Coy. I.30.4, 5 & 6	
			D.Coy. I.30.1, 2 & 3	
			A10 Post ZILLEBEKE	
		8.15pm	Relief complete	
			Casualties: Nil	
	6.2.17		Weather: Very cold.	
		5am	Enemy shelled Rudkin House slightly	
		3&4pm	Our Corps heavy artillery bombarded enemy lines for 1 hour 25 minutes	
		6pm	the Divisional Artillery formed a barrage along the trench. J.19.a.5.w. – J.19.a.3.6. – J.19.a.3.9½. At 6.5 pm the barrage lifted and at 6.10pm firing ceased.	
		6.20pm	The enemy heavily bombarded our front line at I.30.5, 6, 7 & 8 with trench mortars. Retaliation was called for, our artillery did excellent shooting and silenced the enemy.	
			Casualties: Killed 1 O.R. Died of wounds 1 O.R. Wounded 2 O.R. Wounded 2 O.R. on duty 1 O.R.	
	7.2.17		Weather: Very cold	
			Enemy front line was shelled with apparent success	

Army Form C. 2118.

WAR DIARY
or
INTELLIGENCE SUMMARY
(Erase heading not required.)

VOL 2. PAGE 3.

FEBRUARY 1917.

Place	Date	Hour	Summary of Events and Information	Remarks and references to Appendices
	7.2.17		An enemy aeroplane flew over our trench at 7.30.S. at 6.15 p.m. & 9 p.m. Casualties: Nil	
	8.2.17	2 p.m.	Weather: Very cold. Our T.M.s. bombarded enemy trenches in conjunction with our heavies, several of which were falling short. One fell in DAVISON ST and one knocked out two guns of medium T.M. Casualties: Nil.	
	9.2.17		Weather: Very cold. Relieved by the 69th Brigade. At 8.45 p.m. in the middle of the relief the enemy opened a heavy bombardment on our front line. Casualties: Nil.	
	10.2.17	2 a.m.	The Battn. arrived in WINNIPEG CAMP. Casualties: Nil	
WINNIPEG CAMP	11.2.17		Weather: Very cold. Lt Col E.B. Walker went on a C.O.'s course and Captain Every assumed command of the Battn. Casualties: Nil.	
— do —	12.2.17	9.30 a.m. 10.30 a.m.	Weather: Very cold. Major General Babington came to camp. A Brigadier from the Corps visited the camp with Brigadier General Colville. Casualties: Nil.	

Army Form C. 2118.

WAR DIARY
or
INTELLIGENCE SUMMARY
(Erase heading not required.)

Vol 2 PAGE 4
FEBRUARY 1917.

Place	Date	Hour	Summary of Events and Information	Remarks and references to Appendices
MINNIPEG CAMP	13.2.17		Weather: The thaw commenced. Casualties: Nil	
— " —	14.2.17		Weather: Freezing again. Casualties: Nil	
— " —	15.2.17		Weather: Cold. The Batt. bathed at POPERINGHE. Casualties: Nil	
— " —	16.2.17		Weather: The thaw commenced. The Bgde Commander visited the Camp. Casualties: Nil	
— " —	17.2.17	11am	Weather: Still thawing. The Batt. left WINNIPEG CAMP and marched to The BARRACKS, YPRES at 5:30pm relieving 8th YORKS & LANCS. (Lt. Col WATFORD comdg).	
		8.15pm	Relief complete. Casualties: Nil	
THE BARRACKS, YPRES.	18.2.17	3am	Weather: Slight rain. Our guns opened a very heavy bombardment lasting for 1½ hours. Lt. Col C.E. WALKER returned from course. The BARRACKS were shelled slightly during the afternoon & evening. Casualties: Nil	
— " —	19.2.17		Weather: Mild. General CAMERON from Xth Corps visited the BARRACKS. Enemy shelled YPRES throughout the day at odd times and used gas shells in the evening. Gas Alert.	

Army Form C. 2118.

WAR DIARY
or
INTELLIGENCE SUMMARY
(Erase heading not required.)

Vol 2 Page 5
FEBRUARY 1917

Place	Date	Hour	Summary of Events and Information	Remarks and references to Appendices
THE BARRACKS YPRES	20.2.17	5 pm	Weather: Mild & foggy. Our artillery opened a very heavy bombardment; the enemy retaliated a little.	
— " —	21.2.17		Weather: Very foggy. Major J.A.L. Bonney returned from leave. Enemy very quiet.	
— " —	22.2.17		Weather: Very foggy. Relieved 12th Bn. in "A" position. Dispositions:—	
			H. Qrs. TUILLERIES	
			A. Coy WARRINGTON AV.	
			B. Coy 1 Platoon FORT ST	
			" LOVER'S WALK	
			2 Platoons MAPLE ST	
			C. Coy. WELLINGTON CRESCENT.	
			D. Coy RITZ ST	
			Aid Post. ZILLEBEKE	
	23.2.17	10.30 pm	Relief complete. Weather: Foggy.	
		12 noon	Enemy shelled YEOMANRY POST with 5.9's.	
		12.30 pm	Enemy shelled WELLINGTON CRESCENT with 5.9's. Casualties: Nil.	

Army Form C. 2118.

WAR DIARY
or
INTELLIGENCE SUMMARY

(Erase heading not required.)

Vol 2 Page 6.

FEBRUARY 1917.

Instructions regarding War Diaries and Intelligence Summaries are contained in F. S. Regs., Part II. and the Staff Manual respectively. Title Pages will be prepared in manuscript.

Place	Date	Hour	Summary of Events and Information	Remarks and references to Appendices
	24-2-17		Weather: Very foggy. Very quiet all day. The 41st Division raided the enemy result unknown. Casualties: Nil.	
	25-2-17		Weather: Foggy. Quiet all day. Several Officers of 118th Brigade visited H.Qrs. A patrol of 1 officer & 20 O.R. left trench I.24.8. and proceeded S.W. They remained in No Man's Land for one hour and fifteen minutes; no movement by the enemy was seen. Casualties: Wounded 1 O.R.	
	26.2.17		Weather: Fine. One shell fell into H.Qrs.	
		12.30pm to 1.15pm	Enemy shelled WARRINGTON AVENUE.	
			A punishment scheme was put into practice by our artillery. Relieved by 14th SHERWOOD FORESTERS (Major HAUGHTON comdg).	
		11.15pm	Relief complete. Casualties Wounded 2 O.R.	
	27/2/17	4.A.M.	Weather: Fine. Battn arrived in huts at D. Camp A.30.C. The whole day was spent cleaning up for march on 27th & 28th insts. Casualties: Nil.	

Army Form C. 2118.

WAR DIARY
or
INTELLIGENCE SUMMARY

Vol 2. Page 7.
FEBRUARY 1917.

(Erase heading not required.)

Place	Date	Hour	Summary of Events and Information	Remarks and references to Appendices
	28·2·17	9.30am	Weather: Fine. The Battn. left "D" Camp and marched to "Y" camp at F.23.d.2.w. taking over from the 9th Yorkshire Regt. arriving in camp at 12.15 p.m. Casualties: Nil.	

Swalea, Lt. Col.
Comdg. 13th (Serv.) Bn. DURHAM LT. INFTY.

WAR DIARY
or
INTELLIGENCE SUMMARY
(Erase heading not required.)

Army Form C. 2118.
Vol 3   Page 1
March 1917.

13th Durham L.I.

Vol 20

Place	Date	Hour	Summary of Events and Information	Remarks and references to Appendices
BOLLEZEELE	1.3.17	9am	Weather: Mild. The battalion left "Y" Camp and marched to BOLLEZEELE, taking over billets from 10th WEST RIDINGS. The battalion arrived in billets at 4pm. 19 o.r. left but but rejoined. Casualties: Nil	
	2.3.17		Weather: Fine. The whole day was spent cleaning up and rearranging billets. Casualties: Nil	
"	3.3.17		Weather: Fine. Section training under section commanders. Lieut H.P. Markham arrived and was posted to D. Coy. 2/Lieut J.F. Cand arrived and was posted to C. Coy. Casualties: Nil	
"	4.3.17		Weather: Mild. Brigade Church Parade in Square in the morning, and one hour drill in afternoon. Casualties: Nil	
"	5.3.17		Weather: Cold. Training of sections continued. Casualties: Nil	
"	6.3.17		Weather: Cold. Training of sections continued. C.O.'s conference at Divisional Headquarters. Casualties: Nil	
		7.15th		

Army Form C. 2118.

WAR DIARY
or
INTELLIGENCE SUMMARY

(Erase heading not required.)

VOL. 3   PAGE 2.

MARCH 1917.

Instructions regarding War Diaries and Intelligence Summaries are contained in F. S. Regs., Part II. and the Staff Manual respectively. Title Pages will be prepared in manuscript.

Place	Date	Hour	Summary of Events and Information	Remarks and references to Appendices
BOLLEZEELE	7.3.17		Weather: Very cold and high wind. Companies went on a route march in the morning, and continued section training during the afternoon. Casualties: Nil.	
"	8.3.17		Weather: Very cold and snowing. Morning programme was cancelled and companies went for a route march. During the afternoon companies played inter-platoon football matches. Casualties: Nil.	
"	9.3.17		Weather: Very cold and snowed all afternoon. Training continued. Casualties: Nil.	
"	10.3.17		Weather: Mild. Platoon training in morning and recreation during afternoon. Casualties: Nil.	
"	11.3.17		Weather: Very mild. The 12th D.L.I. held sports in the open, while being won by Bn. Bellerby 13th D.L.I. Owing to inoculation there was no training. Casualties: Nil.	
"	12.3.17	2.30pm	Weather: Mild and raining. Training continued. Contact aeroplane practice. The practice was cancelled at 3.15pm owing to mist. Casualties: Nil.	

Army Form C. 2118.

WAR DIARY
or
INTELLIGENCE SUMMARY

(Erase heading not required.)

VOL 3.   PAGE 3.

MARCH 1917

Place	Date	Hour	Summary of Events and Information	Remarks and references to Appendices
BOLLEZEELE	13.3.17		Weather: Mild. Platoon training carried on all day. 2/Lieut. L. Yaneno reported his arrival and posted to E. Coy. Casualties: Nil.	
"	14.3.17		Weather: Mild. Platoon training continued. Baths open to the Battalion.	
		2.30pm	The Brigade Bombing Officer gave a display of a smoke barrage. Casualties: Nil.	
"	15.3.17		Weather: Fine. Training continued during the morning. 13th D.L.I. played 68th R.F. Coy. in the first round of the football Competition; the 13th D.L.I. won 1-0. Casualties: Nil.	
"	16.3.17		Weather: Fine. Platoon training carried on. Casualties: Nil.	
"	17.3.17	9am to 12 noon	Weather: Very fine. Battalion route march. Lt Col G.E. Walker granted 7 days leave; Major J.A.L. Downey assumed Command of Battalion. Casualties: Nil.	

WAR DIARY
or
INTELLIGENCE SUMMARY

Army Form C. 2118.

PAGE 4.

VOL 3

MARCH 1917.

Place	Date	Hour	Summary of Events and Information	Remarks and references to Appendices
BOLLEZEELE	18.3.17		Weather; fine. Raining continued during the morning; recreation during afternoon. Casualties Nil.	
" "	19.3.17	8.30am	Weather; mild. The Battalion paraded in the Square, and at 8-45 am left BOLLEZEELE for HOUTKERQUE.	
		2.30pm	Arrived at destination. One man fell out. The billets were very scattered. Casualties Nil.	
HOUTKERQUE	20.3.17	10am	Weather. Cold and raining. The battalion paraded in front of the Church, HOUTKERQUE and marched to "L" Camp.	
		11.40am	Arrived at destination. Casualties Nil.	
"L" Camp	21.3.17	10.30am	Weather; cold and wet. The Battalion paraded and marched to "E" Camp.	
		12 noon	Arrived at "E" Camp.	
			Captain F.H. Long struck off the establishment.	
"E" Camp	22.3.17	4.30pm	Weather; snowing; wind N. Artillery fire opened on the right sector of 38th Division, to which our artillery immediately retaliated. All quiet at 5am. Captain E.R. Wood struck off the establishment. Casualties Nil.	

Army Form C. 2118.

WAR DIARY
or
INTELLIGENCE SUMMARY

(Erase heading not required.)

VOL. 3. PAGE 5.

MARCH 1917.

Place	Date	Hour	Summary of Events and Information	Remarks and references to Appendices
"E" Camp	23.3.17		Weather: Very cold & windy. Casualties: Nil.	
" "	24.3.17		Weather: Very cold but fine. Found the following working parties in the Battalion. 2 Offrs & 100 O.R. in morning. 5 Offrs & 250 O.R. in evening. Enemy shelled ELVERDINGHE CHATEAU, B.14.a, B.14.c. & B.14.d. with 4.2's where ploughing was going on. Artillery on both sides active all day. Casualties: Nil.	
" "	25.3.17		Weather: Cold & wet. Captain Borrow visited Belgian Lines &c. Working party of 2 Offrs & 200 O.R. found. Casualties: Nil.	
" "	26.3.17		Weather: Cold & wet – cloudy till evening. Very little artillery activity till evening. Found working party of 3 Offrs 10 N.C.Os. and 150 O.R. 2nd Lieut. G.V.W. Sauerbeck reported his arrival reported to C.Coy. Casualties: Nil.	
" "	27.3.17		Weather: Cold, slight showers of hail – Wind N.E. "Situation report and Offensive Patrol and enemy saw few L.H.V. region ESSEX FARM 3.15 p.m. Area Offensive Patrol and Wind N.E." Found working party of 3 Offrs. 10 N.C.Os. and 150 O.R.	
		7pm	Aeroplane activity. Casualties: Nil.	

Army Form C. 2118.

WAR DIARY
or
INTELLIGENCE SUMMARY
(Erase heading not required.)

Vol 3   PAGE 6.

MARCH 1917.

Place	Date	Hour	Summary of Events and Information	Remarks and references to Appendices
"E" Camp	28.3.17		Weather: Clear but cold – wind S.W. No artillery fire on either side. Found working party of 7 Offrs & 340 o.r. Casualties: Nil	
"	29.3.17		Weather: Cloudy and dull. Artillery quiet. Found working party of 7 Offrs & 340 o.r. Casualties: Nil	
"	30.3.17		Weather: Cold and windy with hail showers. Artillery quiet. Found working party of 4 Offrs & 215 o.r. Casualties: Nil	
"	31.3.17		Weather: Cold; hail showers. Artillery quiet. Lt. Col. E.E. Walker returned from leave. Casualties: Nil	

C.J. Walker, Lt: Col:
Comdg 18th (SERV.) Bn. DURHAM LT. INFTY

13 DLI Army Form C. 2118.

VOL 4. PAGE 1.

APRIL 1917.

VOL 21

WAR DIARY
or
INTELLIGENCE SUMMARY.
(Erase heading not required.)

Army Form C. 2118.

Place	Date	Hour	Summary of Events and Information	Remarks and references to Appendices

"E" CAMP	1.4.17		Weather: cold
			Working party found of :-
			  1 Off & 40 O.R.
			  3 Off & 130 O.R.
			Casualties: Nil	

— " —	2.4.17		Weather: cold - rain & sleet
			Artillery quiet
			Working parties found of :-
			  1 Off & 40 O.R.
			  3 Off & 130 O.R.
			Casualties: Nil	

— " —	3.4.17		Weather: Very cold & cloudy
			Working parties found of :-
			  1 Off & 40 O.R.
			  3 Off & 130 O.R.
			     44 O.R.	

— " —	4.4.17		Weather: Snowstorm & windy.
			Working party found. They ceased to during the morning & went out at 1.30pm.
			  3 Off & 150 O.R.
			  1 Off & 40 O.R. billeting tents
			Captain E. Borrow left for Millam in charge of billeting party.
			Casualties: Nil	

— " —	5.4.17	12.25pm	Weather: Fine & warm Left "E" Camp for MILLAM. Arrived at BRANDHOEK at 12.45pm and entrained for ESQUELBECA. Arrived at 3pm. & marched to MILLAM arriving at 6.40pm. Casualties: Nil	

Army Form C. 2118.

WAR DIARY
or
INTELLIGENCE SUMMARY.
(Erase heading not required.)

VOL 4 PAGE 2
APRIL 1917.

Place	Date	Hour	Summary of Events and Information	Remarks and references to Appendices
MILLAM	6.4.17		Weather: Fine. Battalion went for a route march owing to difficulty in obtaining Parade grounds for Companies. Casualties: Nil	
"	7.4.17		Weather: Cold. Captain E. Bonow left for 69th Infy. Brigade on leave to Staff Captain. Casualties: Nil	
"	8.4.17		Weather: Fine. Bombing raid by enemy aircraft carried out in the neighbourhood of Millam. Casualties: Nil	
"	9.4.17		Weather: Wet. Casualties: Nil	
"	10.4.17		Weather: Fair. Company training continued. Casualties: Nil	
"	11.4.17		Weather: Cold. 13th D.L.I. obtained the following awards in the 68th Inf. Bde. Lewis gun competition:- Single Lewis — 1st Prize. Pack Animals — 2nd Prize. Casualties: Nil	
"	12.4.17		Weather: Fine. Company training continued. Casualties: Nil	

Army Form C. 2118.

PAGE 3

WAR DIARY
or
INTELLIGENCE SUMMARY.
(Erase heading not required.)

VOL 4   APRIL 1917.

Place	Date	Hour	Summary of Events and Information	Remarks and references to Appendices
MILLAM	13.4.17		Weather Windy	
		8:30pm	No. 22394 Pte Storey A.Coy tried to swim the canal at MILLAM and was drowned. Pte Ball B.Coy shewed great bravery in trying to save deceased. Casualties: Nil	
" "	14.4.17		Weather Fine	
		6:10am	The Battalion left MILLAM and marched to ESQUELBECQ entraining for POPERINGHE. The Battalion detained at POPERINGHE and marched to Camp at BRANDHOEK.	
		9pm	Advance parties proceeded by train to YPRES to take over the line from the 14th HAMPSHIRE REGT, 116th INFY. BDE. Casualties: Nil	
" "	15.4.17		Weather. Rained hard all day	
		8pm	The Battalion paraded & proceeded to YPRES, relieving 14th HAMPSHIRE REGT. (Lt. Col Hanna B.S.O. comdg.)	
		2am (16.4.17)	Relief completed.	
			Dispositions :- ZILLEBEKE	
			H.Qrs. St Peter St to Cross Tr.	
			A.Coy 2 platoons Winnipeg St Right	
			" 2 " " "	
			C.Coy 1 " Cross Tr.	
			" 2 " Vancouver Tr.	
			" " " Winnipeg St.	
			B.Coy 1 " Sixtieth St	
			" 1 " Fort St	
			" 1 " Hill St (reserve)	
			" 1 " Winnipeg St	

Army Form C. 2118.

PAGE 9.

WAR DIARY
or
INTELLIGENCE SUMMARY.
(Erase heading not required.)

VOL. 4
APRIL 1917

Instructions regarding War Diaries and Intelligence Summaries are contained in F. S. Regs., Part II. and the Staff Manual respectively. Title pages will be prepared in manuscript.

Place	Date	Hour	Summary of Events and Information	Remarks and references to Appendices
	15.4.17		Disposition contd:- B. Coy. Support 2 Platoons CRAB CRAWL dugouts " " 1 " WINNIPEG ST " " " STAFFORD ST AID POST Casualties: Nil	
	16.4.17		Weather: Fine Enemy shelled duck boards near BUND. 3 of H.E's fell into ZILLEBEKE CHURCH. Casualties: Wounded, self inflicted 28856 Pte C. Howley, B. Coy. Wounded, accidental 529114 Pte J. B. Reed D. Coy.	
	17.4.17		Weather: Fine Artillery very quiet all day. During the night the enemy machine guns were very active, and the enemy snipers were active. Casualties: Wounded 1 O.R.	
	18.4.17		Weather: Cold & unsettled. A heavy mist rose during the afternoon. Artillery very quiet Casualties: Nil	
	19.4.17	1.10am (20.4.17)	Weather: Wet 2/Lt F.H.C.D. Smith struck off the strength of Unit on proceeding to England to be transferred to the R.E.A. Relieved by 12th Bat. L.F. in night relief. Relief subject to (Lt. Col. Lyndall comdg.) Relief completed. Disposition:- H.Qrs. RAMPARTS All Coys. BARRACKS.	

Army Form C. 2118.

WAR DIARY
or
INTELLIGENCE SUMMARY.
(Erase heading not required.)

Vol 4 Page 5
APRIL 1917.

Place	Date	Hour	Summary of Events and Information	Remarks and references to Appendices
YPRES	20.4.17		Weather: Fine. Lieut. A.F.B. Howard promoted Captain. 2/Lieut E.R. Heelen promoted Lieutenant. An anti-aircraft shell fell near INFANTRY BARRACKS, YPRES. Casualties: Nil.	
" "	21.4.17		Weather: Fine. Heavy shelling on aerodrome. Captain L.M. Greenwood went to Lewis gun overnight, and proceeded on Adjutants course at CASSEL on 22.4.17. Casualties: Nil.	
" "	22.4.17		Weather: Fine. Casualties: 2/Lt. J. Brady wounded. Wounded 1 O.R.	
" "	23.4.17	8.45 pm 11.30 pm	Weather: Cloudy. Enemy shelled BARRACKS, RAMPARTS and the whole of YPRES generally. also duck boards outside SALLY PORT. Left YPRES, relieving 12th D.L.I. (Lt. Col. Lindale Comdg.) Relief complete. Disposition: H.Q. ZILLEBEKE. A. Coy H.Qs. CRAB CRAWL (deep dugout) 1 Platoon Lepp in YPRES 2 Platoons VANCOUVER ST 1 Platoon WINNIPEG ST (Between ST PETER ST & CRAB CRAWL)	

WAR DIARY or INTELLIGENCE SUMMARY

Army Form C. 2118.

Vol. 4 PAGE 6
APRIL 1917

Place	Date	Hour	Summary of Events and Information	Remarks and references to Appendices
	23.4.17		Disposition - cont'd.	
			B. Co. H.Qrs. CRAB CRAWL (deep dugout)	
			1 platoon CRAB CRAWL	
			" " WINNIPEG (CRAB CRAWL & TOR TOP)	
			" " ST PETER ST.	
			" " With Australian Tunnelling Coy.	
			3 Lewis Guns CRAB CRAWL (deep dugout)	
			C. Co. H.Qrs. CRAB CRAWL (deep dugout)	
			1 platoon VANCOUVER ST.	
			" " CROSS TRENCH	
			" " HILL ST.	
			" " 2nd in C. A. Coy. with Lewis gun.	
			2 Lewis Guns CROSS TRENCH	
			1 Lewis gun VANCOUVER ST.	
			D. Co. H.Qrs. I. 24. a. 3. 7.	
			2 platoons FORT ST.	
			1 platoon BARRACKS, YPRES	
			" " HILL RESERVE	
			1 Lewis gun FORT ST.	
			" " CRAB CRAWL	
			" " HILL 60 ST.	
			" " YPRES	
			All dispositions to be changed on 24.4.17.	
			Casualties: Killed in action 1 O.R.	

Army Form C. 2118.

WAR DIARY
or
INTELLIGENCE SUMMARY.
(Erase heading not required.)

Vol 4 Page 7
April 1917

Place	Date	Hour	Summary of Events and Information	Remarks and references to Appendices

	24.4.17		Weather: Fine. Heavy shelling on both sides. Shells fell on road near Battalion HQrs. also behind. Several aeroplane fights took place. One of our planes came down on fire near the BUND; the occupants not burned but alive. Two aeroplanes were observed to collide and fall behind BODMIN COPSE. Platoon was withdrawn from YPRES. One N.C.O. & six other ranks reported to Town Major, YPRES to take over duties as permanent guards etc. Heavy shelling on WARRINGTON AV. & LEFT FROM HERE to MENIN RD S.O.S. Signal given by 10th Divn. Lieut A.R. Bradshaw went to Bde School on Musketry & L.G. Instruction. New disposition of Batt. carried out as follows on night of 24/25/4 Relief completed 2.25 a.m. 25/4
			
			Battn. H.Qrs. ZILLEBEKE
			A.Coy. 1 Platoon VANCOUVER ST
			     2 Platoons CRAB CRAWL (TOP TOP)
			     2 L.G.s WINNIPEG ST (ST PETER ST)
			     2 L.G.s FRONT LINE
			     Coy. H.Qrs. CRAB CRAWL (deep dugout)
			B.Coy. 1 Platoon CRAB CRAWL (deep dugout)
			     " " FORT ST
			     " " HILL ST
			     2 L.G.s WINNIPEG to VIGO ST
			     1 L.G. CRAB CRAWL
			     Coy H.Qrs. FORT ST
			        CRAB CRAWL	

Army Form C. 2118.

PAGE 8

WAR DIARY
or
INTELLIGENCE SUMMARY.

VOL 4 APRIL 1917

(Erase heading not required.)

Place	Date	Hour	Summary of Events and Information	Remarks and references to Appendices
	22-4-17		Disposition – contd.	
			C. Coy. 2 Platoons — CRAB CRAWL to HILL 60 ST.	
			1 Platoon — CROSS TRENCH	
			1 " — HILL 60 ST.	
			1 L.G. — HILL 60	
			2 L.G.s — CROSS TRENCH	
			1 L.G. — VANCOUVER ST.	
			Coy. H.Qrs. — CRAB CRAWL	
			D. Coy. 3 Platoons — WARRINGTON AV.	
			1 Platoon — LOVERS WALK	
			4 L.G.s — FRONT LINE	
			Coy. H.Qrs. — LOVERS WALK	
			Casualties : Nil	
			Weather : Fine	
	23-4-17	4 a.m.	Own artillery shelled HILL 60 carrying on all day. ZILLEBEKE, BATT H.Qrs., & the TUILERIES shelled with M.G.s and 5.9.s. Heavy shelling by both sides. Aeroplane active. Enemy flew low over front line & was fired on by our L.G.s. Casualties : Wounded R.R. Weather : Fine	
	26-4-17	11 p.m.	Artillery very active on both sides. Barrage put up on sector opposite HILL 60 by us. The enemy retaliated with consult barrage about 20 minutes later.	

Army Form C. 2118.

PAGE 9

WAR DIARY
or
INTELLIGENCE=SUMMARY.

(Erase heading not required.)

Vol 4   APRIL 1917

Place	Date	Hour	Summary of Events and Information	Remarks and references to Appendices
	26-4-17		Continued. Enemy aeroplane flew over our lines at a very low altitude (about 500ft) and was fired on by Lewis guns.	
		6-7.05AM	Our aeroplanes showed great activity. Casualties: Nil	
	27-4-17		Weather: Fine, but rather dull and cold. 2/Lt. P. Owen went to TRANSPORT FARM with 6 o.r. as Bomb Store guard. 70th Infy. Bde. ZILLEBEKE and TUILLERIES Shelled. CRAB CRAWL dugouts inspected by Captain L. Grey and CANADIAN ENGINEER and was certified as being in a clean & sanitary condition. Practised clearing deep dugouts in CRAB CRAWL; every man was out in 4 minutes. Electric bells not good, but new installation being carried out.	

		11.15pm	Battn relieved by 12th D.L.I.
			Relief complete.
			Disposition:-
			    Battn. HQrs. RAMPARTS, YPRES
			    A. Coy INFANTRY BARRACKS
			    B. Coy — do —
			    C. Coy 1 Platoon — do —
			             3 Platoons ESPLANADE DUGOUTS
			    D. Coy CAVALRY BARRACKS
			Casualties: Nil	

WAR DIARY
or
INTELLIGENCE SUMMARY.
(Erase heading not required.)

Army Form C. 2118.

VOL 4 PAGE 10
APRIL 1917

Place	Date	Hour	Summary of Events and Information	Remarks and references to Appendices
Y/PRES	28.4.17		Weather: Fine & warm. Heavy artillery fine. Casualties: Nil.	
" "	29.4.17		Weather: Fine. Heavy artillery fine on both sides. Great aerial activity on both sides. One of our aeroplanes came down behind LOVERS WALK and was shelled with whizzbangs by the enemy. Both occupants rescued by 12th Batt., though badly wounded. Lt Scott of 12th D.L.I. & a Stretcher Bearer attended and got the wounded aviators in to the trench. The S.B. was out about 2 hours & went back three times for assistance. Orders received from Brigade that 19th Division was relieving us on 30th inst. Casualties: Nil.	
" "	30.4.17		Weather: Fine. Heavy artillery fine on left of MENIN Rd. and right of Hill 60 Sector.	
		7.30am	Relieved at YPRES by 6th WILTS REGT.	
		8 am	Batt. moved out in parties of 3 H.Qrs leading & A.B.D.C.	
		10.45am	Advance party left under 2/Lt C. Davies. Whole of Batt. moved out.	
		4⁷pm	Platoons formed up under Platoon Commanders when through VLAMERTINGHE and marched to where cookers were drawn up. Entrained at POPERINGHE. Detrained at GODEWAELDVELD - STEENWOORDE area arriving in billets at 5.45 Am. Casualties: Nil.	

C. Swarts
LT. COL.
COMDG. 13th (SERV.) Bn. DURHAM LT. INFTY.

13 D 4 1

Army Form C. 2118.

VOLUME 5
MAY 1917

PAGE 1

Vol 22

WAR DIARY
or
INTELLIGENCE SUMMARY.
(Erase heading not required.)

Army Form C. 2118.

Place	Date	Hour	Summary of Events and Information	Remarks and references to Appendices
GODEWAERSVELD	1.5.17		Weather: Fine and warm	
		1 a.m.	Heavy artillery fire in sight in the distance about PLOEGSTEERT	
			Hostile aeroplane over.	
			Companies engaged in cleaning billets and baths	
			Casualties : Nil	
"	2.5.17		Weather: Fine and warm	
		10:30 a.m.	L.O. inspected Battalion	
		3:30 p.m.	Major General Sir J. M. Babington inspected the Battalion	
			Casualties : Nil	
"	3.5.17		Weather: Very hot	
			Company and platoon carried on in new formation	
		3.30 p.m.	Enemy aeroplane flew over STEENVOORDE	
			Casualties: Nil	
"	4.5.17		Weather: Very hot	
			Training in open warfare outposts etc.	
			Casualties : Nil	
"	5.5.17		Weather: Very hot	
			Company training carried on	
			Casualties : Nil	
"	6.5.17		Weather: Windy and cold	
		9 a.m.	Church Parade	
		10 a.m.	Demonstration in use of rifle Grenades by 2/5 Lyons. Casualties: Nil.	

Army Form C. 2118.

WAR DIARY
or
INTELLIGENCE SUMMARY.
(Erase heading not required.)

VOLUME 5   PAGE 2
MAY 1917

Place	Date	Hour	Summary of Events and Information	Remarks and references to Appendices
GODEWAERSVELD	7.5.17		Weather :- Fine and hot. Result of Brigade sports :- Tug of war winners 13th D.L.I. Rugby football 11th N.F. v 9th & 13th D.L.I. Nil. Casualties :- Nil.	
"	8.5.17		Weather :- Hot. Bate Boxing Competitions :- Heavy weight won by Pte. Wilson 13th D.L.I. Casualties :- Nil.	
"	9.5.17	9.30am	Weather :- Very hot. The Batt. left STEENVOORDE and marched to SCOTTISH LINES, relieving 7th Batt. S. LANCS REGT. arriving in Camp at 1pm.	
		9.20pm	Our guns in vicinity of YPRES opened a very heavy & intense bombardment ceasing at 10.25pm. Casualties :- Nil.	
SCOTTISH LINES	10.5.17	8.45pm	Weather :- Very hot. The Battalion left SCOTTISH LINES and entrained at BRANDHOEK to relieve 8th NORTH STAFFORDS (left subsector).	
		3.45am	Relief complete. Dispositions :- H.Qrs. Rodkin House Rt Coy A. Coy Gap to 100 yards from Sap G. B. Coy from Left of A. Coy to St Peter St. Left Coy	

Army Form C. 2118.

PAGE 3

WAR DIARY
or
INTELLIGENCE SUMMARY.

VOLUME 5   MAY 1917

Place	Date	Hour	Summary of Events and Information	Remarks and references to Appendices
			Dispositions - contd.	
			SUPPORT Coy. D. Coy. By day OBSERVATORY TR. and REDAN By night 2 platoons held GLASGOW POST and GAP TR.	
			RESERVE Coy. C. Coy. MAPLE TR. and STAFFORD ST.	
	11.5.17		Weather: Hot	
		4.30am	Enemy put several T.M.s into I.30.3 & 4 breaching the parapet opposite centre of CANADA ST. RUDKIN HOUSE was shelled intermittently throughout the day.	
		5 p.m.	Trenches I.30.3 & 4 again shelled with 77mm and T.M.S. Enemy bombarded YPRES and back areas all day. Casualties: Killed 1 o.r. Wounded 4 o.r.	
	12.5.17		Weather: Very hot Enemy artillery was very active all day. RUDKIN HOUSE and the FRONT LINE were shelled, breaching the latter in several places. Casualties: Nil	
	13.5.17		Weather: Hot	
		3.30am	Enemy opened a very heavy bombardment on our trenches in the MOUNT SORRELL Sector.	
		3.45am	Enemy left. Rein trenches in three parties. (1) I.30.3 (2) I.30.4 (3) SAP F. (I.30.5) Berlie party commanded by an officer did not get in. Nos. 1 & 3 parties managed to get into our lines immediately scaled. Strength of parties (1) about 12 (2) about 15 (3) about 20. The second wave about 20 strong only reached half way across	

Army Form C. 2118.

PAGE 4

WAR DIARY
or
INTELLIGENCE SUMMARY.

VOLUME 5 MAY 1917

(Erase heading not required.)

Place	Date	Hour	Summary of Events and Information	Remarks and references to Appendices
	4.5.17		"No man's land" having been stopped by our Lewis Gun fire No. 1. party exited our trenches, but were immediately ejected. The following distinguished themselves by their conspicuous gallantry, coolness and soldierly bearing. 2/Lt. H.C. BUCKELL " E. DAVIS " A.S. HARMER 11324 E.S.M. W.T. Bageley 17750 Sgt. M. Blough 21256 " E. Carter 25503 L/Sgt. G. Lannie 21908 Corp. E. Kirkup 4/27671 " F. McDonnell 13616 L/Corp. Armstrong 3/11640 " A. Harrison 18340 Pte. H. Brankstin 23761 " G. Wrigley 43392 " W.H. Bond Enemy casualties estimated at 18. Casualties:- 7/2/47 E. PARR wounded. Killed 6 o.r. Wounded 13 o.r. Wounded at duty 8 o.r. Missing 1 o.r. Weather: Hot. Two Lewis of Lewises who raided A Coy 13th D.L.I. on 13th inst. see brought in and searched. The Battalion was relieved by 11th NORTHUMBERLAND FUSILIERS	

Army Form C. 2118.

PAGE 5

WAR DIARY
or
INTELLIGENCE SUMMARY
(Erase heading not required.)

VOLUME 5
MAY 1917

Instructions regarding War Diaries and Intelligence Summaries are contained in F.S. Regs., Part II. and the Staff Manual respectively. Title pages will be prepared in manuscript.

Place	Date	Hour	Summary of Events and Information	Remarks and references to Appendices
THE BOND RAILWAY DUGOUTS.		12 midnight	(Lt Col. St Hill Commanding). Relief completed. Dispositions:- H.Qrs. A.B.C & D Coys	
	15.5.17		Weather: Hot Artillery active all day. Our 4.5" Howitzers shelled a new trench in H.14.c.60. sect. Casualties: Nil	
	16.5.17	7 p.m.	Weather: Cloudy and wet. Our artillery very active. Enemy trenches opposite I.33, 34, 35 & 36. were bombarded from 6 p.m. to 6.30 p.m. Lieut. R.B. Holdsworth left the Batt. to rejoin 1/8th D.L.R. Casualties: Nil	
	17.5.17	9.10 p.m. 10.15 p.m. 10.25 p.m.	Weather: raining Artillery fairly quiet. The 12th D.L.I. sent up the S.O.S. at H.14.c.60. sector which was replied to very quickly by our gunners. We blew a small mine opposite MARSHALL POST and SWIFT POST. Received orders to "Stand down". Casualties: Nil	

Army Form C. 2118.

VOLUME 5 PAGE 6
MAY 1917

WAR DIARY
or
INTELLIGENCE SUMMARY.
(Erase heading not required.)

Place	Date	Hour	Summary of Events and Information	Remarks and references to Appendices
	18.5.17		Weather: Fine. Relieved by 11th West Yorks. Dispositions:- H.Qrs, A & B Coys HALIFAX CAMP C & D Coys. BUND The Coys. at the Bund placed under orders of 101st & 102nd Field Coy. R.E. Casualties: Nil	
	19.5.17		Weather: Hot. Provided 4 Offs & 200 men from A & B Coys. to lay cable. Casualties:- Wounded 1 O.R.	
	20.5.17		Weather: Very hot. Draft of 106 o.r. arrived. Casualties: Nil	
HALIFAX CAMP	21.5.17	2.30 pm	Weather: Very hot. Major Gen. Sir J. M. Babington. K.C.M.G., C.B. presented Military Medal ribbon to following :- 13616 A/Cpl G.E. Armstrong 27671 Cpl R. McDonnell 25503 L/Sgt M. Lamie 2376. D/c Tempesby 43392 Pte W.H. Bond 21908 Cpl J.G. Kirkup 11640 L/Cpl A. Harrison 15340 D/c Brankston Casualties:- Wounded 1 O.R.	

Army Form C. 2118.

PAGE 7

WAR DIARY
or
INTELLIGENCE SUMMARY.

VOLUME 5 MAY 1917

(Erase heading not required.)

Place	Date	Hour	Summary of Events and Information	Remarks and references to Appendices
HALIFAX CAMP	22.5.17		Weather: Rain in the morning. Began to clear up after 12am and visibility was better. Casualties: Wounded 3 O.R.	
" "	23.5.17		Weather: Very hot and sultry. C. & D. Coys. relieved by 2 Coys. of 10th N.F. at the BUND.	
		6am	Working parties of the above Coys arrived at HALIFAX CAMP. Casualties: Nil	
" "	24.5.17		Weather: Very hot and sultry. Enemy shelled POPERINGHE. Casualties: Nil	
" "	25.5.17		Weather: Hot. Enemy shelled POPERINGHE. Casualties: Nil	
" "	26.5.17		Weather: Very Hot. No. 21812 Pte. J. Hall awarded the Meritorious Service Medal. The following were mentioned in Despatches. London Gazette 25.5.17. Major G. L. Downey Capt. A.J.B. Havana 3/11324 E.Sm. W.J. Bagley 24747 C.Sm. A. Nichol 22084 P/S R. Harrison Casualties: Nil	

Army Form C. 2118.

PAGE 8

WAR DIARY
or
INTELLIGENCE SUMMARY

(Erase heading not required.)

VOLUME 5

MAY 1917.

Place	Date	Hour	Summary of Events and Information	Remarks and references to Appendices
HALIFAX CAMP	27.5.17		Weather: Very hot. Church parades. Enemy shelled HALIFAX CAMP and R.E. dump intermittently throughout the night. Casualties: Nil.	
— " —	28.5.17		Weather: very hot. Enemy shelled R.E. dump and did a lot of damage to MONTREAL CAMP and the Y.M.C.A. The Battalion left HALIFAX CAMP and moved to St. McADAM CAPPELL Camp H.13.c.5t.2. Following awards:- 2/Lt. H.C. BUCKELL M.C. T/2/Lt. E. DAVIS M.C. C.S.M. W. BAZELEY D.C.M. Sgt. M. BROUGH D.C.M. Casualties: Wounded 3 o.r. Wounded at duty 2 o.r.	
St. McADAM CAPPELL CAMP	29.5.17		Weather: Cold and dull. Brigade Bomb School shelled. Enemy shelled camp again during night. Casualties: Killed 2 o.r. Wounded 7 o.r.	
— " —	30.5.17		Weather: Dull & cool. C.S.M. BAZELEY awarded CROIX DE GUERRE. Casualties: Nil.	

Army Form C. 2118.

PAGE 9

WAR DIARY
or
INTELLIGENCE SUMMARY

Volume 5 May 1917.

(Erase heading not required.)

Place	Date	Hour	Summary of Events and Information	Remarks and references to Appendices
St Mc ADAM CAPPELL CAMP	31-5-17	7.15 p.m.	Weather: Fine. Enemy aeroplane flew over camp. Casualties: Nil.	

J. Irvine Irving
COMDG. 13th (SERV) Bn. DURHAM L.I. IN.T.Y.
Lt. Col. Major

WAR DIARY or INTELLIGENCE SUMMARY

Army Form C. 2118.

13 D L 1 68/23
VOLUME 6 PAGE 1
JUNE 1917.
Vol 23

Place	Date	Hour	Summary of Events and Information	Remarks and references to Appendices
ST MACADAM CAPPELL	1.6.17		Weather: Hot.	
		2 p.m.	The G.O.C. Division presented ribbons to the following:- Captain H.C. Bucknell C.S.M. W.T. Bazeley Sgt. M. Brough Cpl. R. McDonnell Pte. H. Hall	
		8.30 p.m.	Battalion left "O" Camp and relieved 11th Sherwood Foresters in Mount Sorrel sector.	
		11.45 p.m.	Relief complete. Dispositions:- H.Qrs. Rodkin House A. Coy Right Coy B. Coy Left Coy C. Coy Reserve D. Coy Support Enemy artillery was very active during the evening. Brigade St.Qrs. was shelled very heavily, wounding G.O.C. 68th Infy. Bde. Casualties:- S.I.W. 52875 Pte H. Orrell	
	2.6.17		Weather:- Fine Enemy artillery very active all day.	
		10.30 p.m.	Lieut Heselton and 2/Lieut Young attempted a raid on enemy	

Army Form C. 2118.

WAR DIARY
or
INTELLIGENCE SUMMARY
(Erase heading not required.)

VOLUME 6 PAGE 2
JUNE 1917

Place	Date	Hour	Summary of Events and Information	Remarks and references to Appendices
	3.6.17		Weather opposite Saps F. and G. At 10.25 p.m. the enemy opened a very heavy bombardment on Saps F. and G. which disorganised the raiding party. Casualties :- Lieut G.R. HESELTON killed 2/Lieut F. HALL and 2/Lieut G.W. WOOD wounded. 11 o.r. killed and 19 o.r. wounded.	
	4.6.17		Weather : Fine. Very heavy artillery duel all day long. Casualties :- 4 o.r. killed, 12 o.r. wounded and 2 o.r. missing.	
		8.15pm	Weather : Fine. Heavy shelling all day. Battalion H.Q. informed that tomorrow was X day Battalion relieved by the 8th York and Lancs	
		5.30am	Relief complete	
	5.6.17		Casualties :- 1 o.r. accidentally killed	
		9am	Weather : Fine. The Battalion arrived at "O" Camp from the line. The whole day spent resting. Major J.A.L. DOWNEY awarded the D.S.O. Casualties : Nil	

Army Form C. 2118.

PAGE 3

WAR DIARY
or
INTELLIGENCE SUMMARY

VOLUME 6. JUNE 1917

Place	Date	Hour	Summary of Events and Information	Remarks and references to Appendices
"O" Camp	6.6.17		Weather :- Very hot.	
		9.45pm	Captain L. M. GREENWOOD awarded the M.C. The Battalion left "O" Camp and marched into position at south side of ZILLEBEKE LAKE arriving at 11-30 p.m. Night very quiet. Casualties :- 1 O.R. Wounded.	
	7.6.17		Weather : Fine	
		3.10am	The mine under Hill 60 exploded and all the guns in the salient opened fire and 69th and 70th Brigades attacked.	
		9.15am	A. and B. Coys moved up to BATTERSEA FARM and came under orders of G.O.C. 69th Brigade.	
		10pm	H.Qrs, A. and B. Coys. were sent for to relieve 12th D.L.I. in IMPARTIAL TRENCH.	
	8.6.17	5am	Relief completed. Casualties :- 1 O.R. Killed, 4 O.R. Wounded and 1 O.R. missing.	
	8.6.17		Weather : Fine Fairly quiet during the day.	
		8.20pm	An aeroplane flew over our lines and dropped a white light; our artillery immediately opened a very heavy bombardment	

WAR DIARY
or
INTELLIGENCE SUMMARY

(Erase heading not required.)

Army Form C. 2118.

VOLUME 6 PAGE 4
JUNE 1917

Place	Date	Hour	Summary of Events and Information	Remarks and references to Appendices
	9.6.17		Lasting till 10 p.m. Battalion H.Q. was heavily shelled. Casualties :- 2/Lieut. J. Young Killed. 2/Lieut. J. Brady wounded. 3 O.R. killed, 25 O.R. wounded and 1 O.R. missing. Weather : Fine	
		4.30am	C. Coy moved up and relieved 1 Coy of 12th D.L.I. in RECTANGLE and B. Coy relieved 2 Coys of 12th D.L.I. in BATTERSEA FARM.	
		10.30am	Front Line heavily shelled	
		11pm	B. Coy moved up and relieved 2 Coys. 11th WEST YORKS Casualties :- 20 O.R. killed 18 O.R. wounded	
	10.6.17		Weather : Fine	
		2am	C. Coy and 1 Coy SOUTH STAFFORDS dug a support line about 50 yards behind IMPARTIAL TRENCH naming same DURHAM LANE Dispositions :- H.Qrs. I. 29. d. 7. 4. A. & D. Coys. IMPARTIAL TR. C. Coy DURHAM LANE B. Coy IMPRESERVE and 13th AVENUE. C. Coy shelled intermittently all day. Telephonic communication established between Batn. H.Q. & Coys. Casualties :- 2/Lieut. A. HAMILTON Killed, 2/Lieut. T. MURGATROYD wounded 3 O.R. killed and 30 O.R. wounded.	

Army Form C. 2118.

PAGE 5

WAR DIARY
or
INTELLIGENCE SUMMARY

(Erase heading not required.)

VOLUME 6 JUNE 1917

Place	Date	Hour	Summary of Events and Information	Remarks and references to Appendices
	11.6.17		Weather: Dull and rain at intervals. Enemy shelled front line and Batt. H.Q. heavily, at odd times throughout the day.	
		10.40pm to 11.40pm	Enemy heavily shelled our front line and support line and 47th Div. front. Our artillery opened a very heavy barrage immediately. Casualties: 1 o.r. killed. 16 o.r. wounded and 6 o.r. missing.	
	12.6.17		Weather: Fine. D. Coys Post in RAILWAY DUGOUTS was bombed and all the garrison became casualties.	
		12.15am	After a Stokes mortar preparation LIEUT T.G. SAINT and a party of bombers went out and was again attacked and driven back as far as junction of IMMEDIATE DRIVE and IMPARTIAL TRENCH. LIEUT SAINT counter attacked and regained his Post. Our heavies were very active all day.	
		8.30pm	Received orders from 69th Bde. to occupy and hand over Post at I.36.c.3.0. Relieved by 12th Royal Fusiliers 24th Division. Enemy opened a heavy bombardment and kept it up all night. Casualties:- LIEUT T.G. SAINT wounded 2 o.r. killed 5 o.r. wounded	

Army Form C. 2118.

WAR DIARY
or
INTELLIGENCE SUMMARY

Volume 6 Page 6
June 1917

(Erase heading not required.)

Place	Date	Hour	Summary of Events and Information	Remarks and references to Appendices
Mont-des-Cats	13.6.17	3.30 a.m.	Weather: Very fine. Relief completed. Battalion marched to VLAMERTINGHE and entrained by 7 a.m. Detrained at GODEWAERSVELDE at 9 a.m. Day spent resting.	
"	14.6.17		Weather very hot. The Battalion rested all day. Casualties: Nil.	
"	15.6.17		Weather: Very hot. G.O.C. Division inspected the Brigade. Casualties: Nil.	
"	16.6.17		Weather: Extraordinarily hot. Company training carried on. Casualties: Nil.	
"	17.6.17		Weather: Very hot. Church Parades held in the morning and cricket match in the afternoon against the Second Army Sniping School. Casualties: Nil.	
"	18.6.17		Weather: Heavy thunderstorm. Casualties: Nil.	

Army Form C. 2118.

WAR DIARY
or
INTELLIGENCE SUMMARY
(Erase heading not required.)

VOLUME 6   PAGE 7
JUNE 1917

Place	Date	Hour	Summary of Events and Information	Remarks and references to Appendices
MONT-DES-CATS	19.6.17		Weather: Very hot. Cricket match was played versus "Z" Special Coy R.E. 13th D.L.I. winning easily. Casualties: Nil	
"	20.6.17		Weather: Very hot. The Battalion bathed. Casualties: Nil	
"	21.6.17		Weather: Cold and raining. Pte Page D. Coy presented with Military Medal. Casualties: Nil	
"	22.6.17		Weather: Heavy thunderstorm. Training stopped owing to the rain. Casualties: Nil	
"	23.6.17		Weather: Wet. Brigade Horse show was held in the morning, the Transport obtaining 1 first prize and 2 second prizes. Captain DUNNWATERS demonstrated with the Yukon Pack at Bde. HQrs. Casualties: Nil	
"	24.6.17		Weather: Very clear and fine. Church Parades. Casualties: Nil	

Army Form C. 2118.

WAR DIARY
or
INTELLIGENCE SUMMARY
(Erase heading not required.)

VOLUME 6. PAGE 8
JUNE 1917

Place	Date	Hour	Summary of Events and Information	Remarks and references to Appendices
MONT DES CATS	25.6.17		Weather: Fine. 23rd Divl. Horse Show held. Casualties: Nil	
"	26.6.17		Weather: Fine. The G.O.C. Division presented medal ribbons to the Brigade. After the inspection the Brigade Bombing Officer gave a demonstration of use of rifle grenade. Casualties: Nil	
"	27.6.17		Weather: Very heavy rain. Company training continued. Casualties: Nil	
"	28.6.17		Weather: Rain. Coys. went for an 8 mile route march. Army Commander inspected the Brigade during the afternoon. Casualties: Nil	
"	29.6.17		Weather: Rain. Coys. went for a 9 mile route march during the morning. Casualties: Nil	
"	30.6.17	6 a.m.	Weather: Rainy all day. The Battalion moved from Mont-Des-Cats by motor lorries and arrived at MICMAC CAMP at 12.30 p.m. Casualties: Nil	

g. Louis Vann
Lt-Col:Major
COMDG. 13th (SERV.) Bn. DURHAM Lt. INFTY.

Vol 24

13th (S) Battalion Durham Light Infantry.

WAR DIARY

VOLUME 4. JULY 1919

From O/C 13th (S) Battn. Durham L.I.

To. H.Q. 68th Infantry Brigade.

        Herewith War Diary for the month of July. 1917.

1.8.17.

                        D.T.Clarke Capt.

                      COMDG. 13th (SERV.) Bn. DURHAM Lt. INFTY.

WAR DIARY or INTELLIGENCE SUMMARY.

(Erase heading not required.)

Army Form C. 2118.

VOLUME 7. PAGE 1.
JULY 1917

Place	Date	Hour	Summary of Events and Information	Remarks and references to Appendices
MICMAC CAMP	1.7.17		Enemy shelled MICMAC CAMP and district around it at intervals during the day. Casualties NIL	
	2.7.17	1.15am	3 Shells dropped near the Camp	
		2.15am	2 Shells dropped near the Camp	
		3.15am	3 Shells dropped near the Camp	
			Enemy Aircraft very active all day.	
	3.7.17		Received a Draft of 34 O.R. Average age 32.	
	4.7.17	3.00am	Enemy dropped a few Bombs from an Aeroplane near MICMAC CAMP causing a few casualties in R.A.	
		9.0am	His Majesty the King passed along the LA CLYTE - RENINGHELST ROAD	
			A Draft of 40 O.R. arrived.	
			"B" and "C" Coys left Camp and relieved 2 Coys of 8th York & Lancs Regt.	
			Dispositions "B" Coy CANADA ST. "C" Coy METROPOLITAN LEFT.	

Army Form C. 2118.

PAGE 2

WAR DIARY
or
INTELLIGENCE SUMMARY.

VOLUME 7   JULY 1917.

(Erase heading not required.)

Place	Date	Hour	Summary of Events and Information	Remarks and references to Appendices
	5/7/17		A Draft of 12 O.R arrived from the Base	
			35 O.R proceeded to BATTERSEA FARM and formed a Composite Coy under	
			an Officer of 11th NORTHUMBERLAND FUSILIERS.	
		10:15am	Conference of all officers at each Brigade Headquarters by Major General	
			Sir J.M. BABINGTON, K.C.M.G. C.B. The C.R.E explained what work was to	
			be done in the line	
		8:30pm	The Battalion left MICMAC CAMP and proceeded to relieve 2nd K.O.Y.L.I	
			in front line	
			Casualties 2 O.R Wounded.	
	6/7/17	1:15am	Relief complete.	
			Dispositions. MAP HILL 60	
			Headquarters. I 29 d 6.4.	
			"C" Company I 36 b 2 3 to I 36 b 5 8	
			"B" Company I 36 b 5 8 to I 30 d 15.50	
			"D" Company I 30 c 4 6 6 6.	
			"A" Company I 29 d 4.4.	

WAR DIARY
INTELLIGENCE SUMMARY.

(Erase heading not required.)

Army Form C. 2118.
VOLUME 7 PAGE 3
JULY 1917

Place	Date	Hour	Summary of Events and Information	Remarks and references to Appendices
		1·30am	A small reconnoitering party went out from the right of our line about I.36.b.45.35 Enemy machine Guns intermittently swept gaps in new trench from I.36.c.25.10 to I.36.b.5.9. Casualties 1 O R wounded.	
	7.7.17	12.15am	A patrol consisting of 2/Lieut F YOUENS and 3 OR left the night of 43Ltn front to get into touch with the 19th LONDON REGT. They then proceeded to about I.36.b.51 where a party of about 40 of the enemy was observed carrying material into the Strong Point. The enemy covering party tried to surround the patrol and after a Bombing fight our patrol was forced to retire 2/Lieut F YOUENS and 1 OR being wounded	
		1·45am 3·0am	Enemy shelled front and support lines very heavily	
		2·30am	A party of about 50 Germans attempted to raid the Right Coy. at I.36.b.5.8. They were repulsed by Rifle and Lewis Gun fire. 2/Lieut. F. YOUENS although wounded came out of the dug-out without tunic or Shirt and rallied a Lewis Gun team which had been disorganised by a Shell. The enemy threw a bomb into the centre of this Lewis	

WAR DIARY

VOLUME 4   PAGE 4.

INTELLIGENCE SUMMARY.   JULY 1917.

(Erase heading not required.)

Army Form C. 2118.

Place	Date	Hour	Summary of Events and Information	Remarks and references to Appendices
			Run Yeam and 2/Lieut F.YOUENS caught hold of it and threw it away. The enemy did throw a second time and as 2/Lieut F.YOUENS was throwing the second bomb away, it burst and badly wounded him. Enemy Artillery normal throughout the day on front line but very active round Headquarters. Casualties 2/Lieut. F.YOUENS Wounded. 3 O.R. Killed - in - Action. 12 O.R. Wounded.	
	8.7.17		Weather. Very Wet. Enemy Artillery very active in bursts of heavy firing every 3/4 of an hour firing from the direction of HOOGE and ZANDVOORDE. Casualties 1 O.R. killed - in Action. 1 O.R. Wounded.	
	9.7.17	12.30am	An Officer's Patrol left Trench at I.36.6.2.4. An Enemy Party of about 40 was observed at I.36.6.45.35. Own party was fired on by Enemy's Covering Party. The Patrol returned, and a Lewis Gun fired on	

WAR DIARY

INTELLIGENCE SUMMARY.

VOLUME 4   PAGE 5

Army Form C. 2118.

JULY 1917.

(Erase heading not required.)

Place	Date	Hour	Summary of Events and Information	Remarks and references to Appendices
			Enemy's party. Result indefinite. Enemy returned to his trenches.	
		10·0am	Whole area heavily shelled for 1/4 of an hour. Battalion Headquarters was heavily shelled about once every hour.	
		10·30pm	Battalion relieved by 12th Battalion Durham Light Infantry. Casualties 1 O.R. Wounded	
	10.7.17	3·0am	Relief Complete. The Battalion withdrew to MICMAC CAMP.	
MICMAC CAMP	11.7.17		Lt. Col. M. E. LINDSAY D.S.O. 9th Dragoon Guards rejoined Battalion and assumed Command	
	12.7.17	5·0pm	Two Enemy Aeroplanes flew near the Camp. Our Lewis Guns fired and drove them off the Camp. Casualties 2 O.R. Wounded	
	13.7.17	3·0am	Enemy Aeroplane dropped 3 Bombs near the Camp. No damage was done.	
			2/Lieut A. E. TURNER M.C. and 2/Lieut W. C. HODGSON reported their arrival	
	14.7.17		G.O.C. 23rd Division presented ribbons to the following	

WAR DIARY

VOLUME M PAGE 6 Army Form C. 2118.

INTELLIGENCE SUMMARY.

JULY 1919

Place	Date	Hour	Summary of Events and Information	Remarks and references to Appendices
			T/Capt E. GRAY — M.C.	
			T/Capt L.M GREENWOOD — M.C	
			T/Lieut C.T.W. SAUERBECK — M.C	
			52644 C.S.M. G THOMPSON — D.C.M	
			13820 Private I. PAIN — M.M	
			20939 Private T. CLARKE — M.M	
	15.7.19		Lieut y. C SAINT returned to Battalion and posted to 'D' Coy	
	16.7.19		2/Lieut. G TAYLOR reported his arrival and posted to 'A' Coy	
	17.7.19		Draft of 14 O.R arrived	
	17.7.19		Working Party of 120 O.R carried SAA for 10th machine Gun Coy	
	18.7.19		Enemy Artillery active in rear areas several shells falling near the Camp	
Sheet 28 NW H 21 d 9.1	19.7.19		Owing to enemy night shelling the Camp was moved to H.21 d.9.1	
	20.7.19		Enemy Aircraft active during the day	
MONT DES CATS	21.7.19		The Battalion paraded at 7-15 am and proceeded by march Route to MONT DES CATS arriving in Billets at 12-0 noon 3 men fell out	

WAR DIARY VOLUME 4 Page 7

INTELLIGENCE SUMMARY. JULY 1919

Army Form C. 2118.

Place	Date	Hour	Summary of Events and Information	Remarks and references to Appendices
MONT DES CATS	22/7/19		Church Parade. Remainder of day spent in cleaning up	
	23/7/19		Company Training. Enemy Aircraft dropped Bombs near MONT DES CATS during the night.	
	24/7/19		G.O.C. 23rd Division inspected the Battalion and presented the D.C.M. Ribbon to 15594 C.S.M. G. WOODRUFF.	
	25/7/19		Company Training	
	26/7/19		Company Training. 2/Lieut E.C. FORREST and 2/Lieut W.T. CALDWELL reported and posted to "B" and "C" Coys respectively	
	27/7/19		Company Training	
	28/7/19		Brigade Sports. Battalion won 6 out of 8 events	
	29/7/19		Rained heavily preventing Church Parade. Lt. Col M.E. LINDSAY D.S.O proceeded on leave.	
	30/7/19		The Battalion left MONT DES CATS at 12.0 noon and entrained at CAESTRE at 3.40 pm arriving at ST OMER at 11.15 pm the Battalion arrived in Billets at WIZERNES at 1.0 am on 31st.	

WAR DIARY VOLUME 4. PAGE 8. Army Form C. 2118.
or
INTELLIGENCE SUMMARY. JULY 1917.

(Erase heading not required.)

Place	Date	Hour	Summary of Events and Information	Remarks and references to Appendices
WIZERNES.	31/7/17		Company training Carried on.	
			2/Lt R.W. GILL reported this arrival and posted to 'C' Coy.	

D.H.Clarke
Capt.
Lt.Col.
COMDG: 13th (SERV.) Bn. DURHAM Lt. INFTY.

WAR DIARY
INTELLIGENCE SUMMARY
(Erase heading not required.)

Army Form C. 2118.

VOL VIII PAGE 1.
AUGUST 1917.

Vol 25

Place	Date	Hour	Summary of Events and Information	Remarks and references to Appendices
WIZERNES	1.8.17		Weather :- Rained heavily. G.O.C. Division visited the Battalion.	
-"-	2.8.17		Weather :- Rained heavily. Heavy rain again prevented training.	
-"-	3.8.17		Weather :- Rained. A concert was held in D. Coys billet. The following Officers reported their arrival & were posted to the following Coys:- 2/Lt R.W.GULL C.Coy 2/Lt L. BENLEY D.Coy Casualties :- Nil	
-"-	4.8.17		2/Lt F. YOVENS (Died of wounds) awarded Victoria Cross for conspicuous gallantry. 2/Lt H.K. JACKSON reported his arrival and posted to A.Coy. Draft of 10 o.r. arrived Casualties :- Nil	

WAR DIARY
or
INTELLIGENCE SUMMARY. Vol VIII   Page 2

August 1917.

Place	Date	Hour	Summary of Events and Information	Remarks and references to Appendices
WIZERNES	5.8.17		Football match between Officers and Sergeants. The Sergeants winning by 2 goals to nil. Casualties :- Nil	
"	6.8.17		Company training on the training area.	
		10.30pm	All Officers recalled from leave. Casualties :- Nil	
"	7.8.17		The Army Commander inspected the Battalion on the training area. Casualties :- Nil	
"	8.8.17		2/Lt W.J. ARRIS won the Officers' revolver competition. In the Brigade Boxing competition the 13th D.L.I. won (1) Heavy weight (2) Welter weight (3) Feather weight 13th D.L.I. played 71st F.A. at Cricket and won by 3 runs. Casualties :- Nil	

Army Form C. 2118.

WAR DIARY
or
INTELLIGENCE SUMMARY.

VOL. VIII PAGE 3
AUGUST 1917

(Erase heading not required.)

Place	Date	Hour	Summary of Events and Information	Remarks and references to Appendices
WIZERNES	9.8.17		The Battalion left WIZERNES and proceeded by march route to MOULLE arriving at 12 noon. Casualties :- Nil.	
MOULLE	10.8.17		The G.O.C. Division inspected C. Coy. at training. Casualties :- Nil.	
" "	11.8.17		The XVIIIth Corps Commander lectured to C.O. and Company Commanders at HOUEE. Casualties :- Nil.	
" "	12.8.17		Church Parade in Y.M.C.A. hut. C. D. Boys fired on troops in afternoon. Casualties :- Nil.	
" "	13.8.17		Night operations by 68th Brigade. A compass march for officers afterwards. Casualties :- Nil.	
" "	14.8.17		No work in afternoon. Xth Corps School Yorks Lela. Casualties :- Nil.	

WAR DIARY
INTELLIGENCE SUMMARY
(Erase heading not required.)

Army Form C. 2118.

Vol VIII   PAGE 4
August 1917

Place	Date	Hour	Summary of Events and Information	Remarks and references to Appendices
MOULLE	15-8-17		Demonstration by 62nd Trench Mortar Battery.	
"	16-8-17		LIEUT A.J.L. PARKER reported his arrival & posted to D. Coy. Casualties :- Nil	
"			Company training on TILQUES training area. Casualties :- Nil	
"	17-8-17		Company training continued. Weather very hot. Casualties :- Nil	
"	18-8-17		Weather very hot. A & B. Coys. fired on range. Casualties :- Nil	
"	19-8-17		Church parade. Water gala held by 10th N.F. at SERQUES Casualties :- Nil	
"	20-8-17		Battalion scheme on training area. Ground converted by flags etc to represent portion of ground near POELCAPELLE. 2/LIEUT H.C. SEBBORN reported his arrival & posted to A. Coy. Casualties :- Nil	

Army Form C. 2118.

WAR DIARY
or
INTELLIGENCE SUMMARY.   Vol VIII   PAGE 5
AUGUST 1917
(Erase heading not required.)

Instructions regarding War Diaries and Intelligence Summaries are contained in F. S. Regs., Part II. and the Staff Manual respectively. Title pages will be prepared in manuscript.

Place	Date	Hour	Summary of Events and Information	Remarks and references to Appendices
MOULLE	21.8.17		Company bombing section practised throwing with live bombs. Casualties :- Nil	
" "	22.8.17		Brigade scheme over ground as on 20.8.17. 2/Lt. F.E.C.D. SMITH reported his arrival & posted to B.Coy. Weather very hot. Casualties :- Nil	
" "	23.8.17		Field firing practice by C & D Coys at GUEMY. Transport left for OUDERDOM by road. Casualties :- Nil	
" "	24.8.17 8am	The Battalion left MOULLE entraining at WATTEN at 12 noon, detrained at RENINGHELST at 4.30 pm and arrived in PALACE CAMP H.25.c.4.0. at 5.30 p.m. Casualties :- Nil	
PALACE CAMP	25.8.17		Officers & N.C.O.s visited the "Place of Lincles" on the BUSSEBOOM RD. Casualties :- Nil	

WAR DIARY
or
INTELLIGENCE SUMMARY. Vol. VIII

(Erase heading not required.)

Army Form C. 2118.

PAGE 6
1 AUGUST 1917.

Place	Date	Hour	Summary of Events and Information	Remarks and references to Appendices
PALACE CAMP	26.8.17		Church Parade. Casualties:- Nil	
-"-	27.8.17		Weather very wet. Casualties:- Nil	
-"-	28.8.17		MAJOR J.M. LONGDON reported his arrival and assumed the duties of 2nd in command. Casualties:- Nil	
-"-	29.8.17		Weather very wet.	
		6pm	The Battalion moved from PALACE CAMP and marched to camp at DICKEBUSCH at H.33.c.7.3. Camp is in a very bad condition. Casualties:- Nil	
DICKEBUSCH	30.8.17		Weather dull. Companies marched to the "model of trenches" Casualties:- Nil	

Army Form C. 2118.

PAGE 7.

WAR DIARY
or
INTELLIGENCE SUMMARY.

(Erase heading not required.)

Vol. VIII   AUGUST 1917.

Place	Date	Hour	Summary of Events and Information	Remarks and references to Appendices
DICKEBUSCH	31-8-17	2.05 pm	Enemy aeroplanes dropped bombs in the vicinity of the camp and HALLEBAST CORNER where a great deal of damage was done.	
			Casualties: 2 O.R. wounded at duty.	

W. Lindsay Lt. Col.
COMDG: 13th (SERV.) Bn. DURHAM Lt. INFY.

CONFIDENTIAL.

WAR DIARY

of

13th.(S) BATTALION, THE DURHAM LIGHT INFANTRY.

From.   1st Sept. 1917.

To.   30th Sept. 1917.

Army Form C. 2118.

WAR DIARY
or
INTELLIGENCE SUMMARY.
(Erase heading not required.)

VOL. IX PAGE 1 SEPTEMBER 1917

Place	Date	Hour	Summary of Events and Information	Remarks and references to Appendices
DICKEBUSCH	1.9.17		Weather hot. Enemy shelled DICKEBUSCH	
"	2.9.17	9.20 p.m	The Battalion moved from DICKEBUSCH H.33 a.7.3. to billets at STEENVOORDE arriving at 4.30 p.m.	
"	3.9.17	1 a.m	Enemy aircraft very active. Bombs were dropped near STEENVOORDE during the night 2/3rd. Weather very hot.	
STEENVOORDE	4.9.17		Weather very hot. Training carried out under Company arrangements.	
"	5.9.17		The Battalion moved from STEENVOORDE and marched to NOORDPEENE arriving at 2.5 p.m. The billets were very scattered.	
NOORDPEENE	6.9.17		Weather very hot in the morning. Thunderstorm at 6 p.m.	
"		2.30 p.m	C.O's conference at Brigade H.Q.	
"	7.9.17		Training carried on in Company areas	
"	8.9.17		Weather very hot	

Army Form C. 2118.

WAR DIARY
or
INTELLIGENCE SUMMARY.
(Erase heading not required.)

Vol. IX   PAGE 2   SEPTEMBER 1917

Place	Date	Hour	Summary of Events and Information	Remarks and references to Appendices
NOORDPEENE	9.9.17		Weather very hot. Church parade.	
"	10.9.17	10am	Company Commanders' conference. Weather very hot. Company training in billet area.	
		1.45pm	3 haystacks near B.Coy. caught fire. Court of enquiry was held. President:— Major J.M. LONGDEN Members:— 2/Lt. G. TAYLOR, 2/Lt. C.H. ROLLSTON	
"	11.9.17		Weather very hot. Casualties:— Capt. C.T.W. SAUERBECK M.C. killed in action.	
"	12.9.17		Weather very hot. Brigade operations at MENEGAY.	
"	13.9.17	1.40pm	The Battalion left NOORDPEENE and proceeded to STEENVOORDE by march route arriving at 6.30pm.	

WAR DIARY or **INTELLIGENCE SUMMARY.**
(Erase heading not required.)

Army Form C. 2118.

VOL. IX PAGE 3
SEPTEMBER 1917

Place	Date	Hour	Summary of Events and Information	Remarks and references to Appendices
STEENVOORDE	14.9.17	7.15am	The Battalion left STEENVOORDE and proceeded by march route to CHIPPAWA CAMP M.6.a.2.7. pluss 28. S.W. relieving the 14th HANTS. 39th DIVISION. Enemy aircraft very active.	
CHIPPAWA CAMP	15.9.17			
	16.9.17	8.30am	The Battalion left CHIPPAWA CAMP and marched to DICKEBUSCH arriving at 9.30am at H.33.a.7.3. Dickebusch was shelled.	
		10.30pm	A very heavy bombardment was heard.	
		10.45am	17 enemy aeroplanes flew over the camp including 2 GOTHAS. Bombs were dropped at OUDERDOM.	
DICKEBUSCH	17.9.17		Weather fait. G.O.C. Division visited the camp.	
	18.9.17		Dull and rainy. The Battalion was put through a gas demonstration. Casualties :- 1 O.R. wounded.	

Army Form C. 2118.

PAGE 1
VOL IX SEPTEMBER 1917

WAR DIARY
or
INTELLIGENCE SUMMARY.
(Erase heading not required.)

Instructions regarding War Diaries and Intelligence Summaries are contained in F. S. Regs., Part II. and the Staff Manual respectively. Title pages will be prepared in manuscript.

Place	Date	Hour	Summary of Events and Information	Remarks and references to Appendices
DICKEBUSCH	19.9.17	11am	The Battalion left camp at DICKEBUSCH under the command of CAPTAIN D.H. CLARKE M.C. and marched to RAILWAY DUGOUTS and halted there till 4.45 p.m. when they moved up to assembly trenches at TORR TOP. Lt Col M.E. LINDSAY D.S.O. proceeded on leave. Casualties:- 3 O.R. Wounded	
	20.9.17	3am	Battalion H.Q. moved to Advanced Brigade H.Q at T.19.T.10.25.	
		5.40am	At ZERO hour the Battalion moved forward to JAM area trenches	
		7.30am	Battalion moved forward from JAM area arriving on the BLUE LINE at 8.50 am.	
		9am	Battalion H.Q. established at J.20.B.7.4.	
		9.53am	The Battalion advanced from the BLUE LINE to attack the GREEN LINE	
		10.40am	German prisoners passed Battalion H.Q. about 150 in all	
		11.5am	The GREEN LINE was captured and consolidation in progress.	

Army Form C. 2118.

PAGE 5
VOL IX SEPTEMBER 1917

WAR DIARY
or
INTELLIGENCE SUMMARY.
(Erase heading not required.)

Place	Date	Hour	Summary of Events and Information	Remarks and references to Appendices
	20.9.17		continued	
		3pm	About 100 of the enemy attacked the Left Company and were dispersed.	
			Casualties — Killed — CAPT. H.C. BUCKELL M.C. and 44 O.R.	
			Wounded — LIEUT. H.J.L. PARKER, 2/Lt. R.W. GILL, 2/Lt. H.R. WHEATLEY, 2/Lt. G.L. ORCHARD and 174 O.R. — Missing — 16 O.R.	
	21.9.17	4.30AM	Our artillery opened a very heavy barrage till 5.15 a.m.	
		5am	Enemy again attacked the Left Company and were dispersed by our Lewis gun and rifle fire. 1 German officer and 5 O.R. captured.	
		3pm	After an heavy bombardment the enemy attacked the Right Company up the valley from GHELUVELT; they were again dispersed.	
		4pm	After two hours heavy shelling the enemy were seen massing on the right of the YPRES – MENIN ROAD near GHELUVELT preparatory to attacking.	

Army Form C. 2118.

PAGE 6.

WAR DIARY
or
INTELLIGENCE SUMMARY.
(Erase heading not required.)

VOL. IX SEPTEMBER 1917

Place	Date	Hour	Summary of Events and Information	Remarks and references to Appendices
	21.9.17		continued	
			The S.O.S. signal was sent up on our right and left and the enemy were caught by our barrage before his attack could materialise.	
			Remainder of the night was quiet.	
			Casualties :- Killed - 14 O.R. Wounded - 37 O.R. Missing - 10 O.R.	
	22.9.17	3 a.m.	Two Companies of the 8th K.O.Y.L.I. relieved the Battalion which withdrew to YORK TOP dugouts with the exception of H.Qrs. and 2 platoons of B. Company who were relieved at dusk.	
			Casualties :- Killed - 1 O.R. Wounded - 5 O.R. Missing - 1 O.R.	
	23.9.17	7.30 a.m.	The Battalion withdrew to camp at DICKEBUSCH	
			Casualties :- Wounded - 1 O.R. Missing - 1 O.R.	
DICKEBUSCH	24.9.17	10.5 a.m.	The Battalion left DICKEBUSCH and marched to YORK CAMP, WESTOUTRE arriving at 12 noon.	
			The following letter was received from 33rd D.A.	

WAR DIARY
INTELLIGENCE SUMMARY

Army Form C. 2118.

PAGE 7
VOL IX
SEPTEMBER 1917

Place	Date	Hour	Summary of Events and Information	Remarks and references to Appendices
	24.9.17		*Continued*	
			"To O.C. 13th D.A.I.	
			We of the 33rd D.A. cannot let you go out without	
			wishing you the best of luck & giving you our heartiest	
			congratulations. All our F.O.O's, B.C. and all are full of	
			the 13th D.A.I. & we all look on you as our own Infantry.	
			We all hope that we may again have the honour of	
			supporting you & doing still more for you. We have	
			had the best of good hunting together. I hope you	
			will go off thinking even half as much of the 33rd D.A.	
			as they do of you.	
			Sd Bernard Ballel Lt Col R.A.	
			Cdg 156 Bde R.F.A.	
			33rd D.A."	
	23.9.17			
YORK CAMP	25.9.17	11.15a.m.	The G.O.C. inspected the Battalion.	
WESTOUTRE	26.9.17		Weather very hot.	

Army Form C. 2118.

WAR DIARY
or
INTELLIGENCE SUMMARY.
(Erase heading not required.)

VOL. IX PAGE 8
SEPTEMBER 1917

Place	Date	Hour	Summary of Events and Information	Remarks and references to Appendices
YORK CAMP, WESTOUTRE	27.9.17		Major J.M. LONGDEN attached to 11 R.N.F.	
"	28.9.17	10.35am	Captain D.H. CLARKE M.C. assumed command of the Battalion. The Battalion moved to ASCOT CAMP arriving at 10.50 a.m. Enemy aircraft very active all night. Casualties:- Wounded – 2 o.r. Died of wounds – 1 o.r.	
ASCOT CAMP, WESTOUTRE	29.9.17		100 men of B. Company sent on a working party to RAILWAY DUGOUTS. Enemy aircraft again very active dropping bombs.	
"	30.9.17		The Officers of 13th D.L.I. played 68th M.G.C. at soccer. Result 2 goals each.	

D.H. Clarke.
Lt-Col. Captain.
COMDG: 13th (SERV.) Bn. DURHAM LT. INFTY.

Army Form C. 2118.

WAR DIARY
or
INTELLIGENCE SUMMARY.
(Erase heading not required.)

PAGE 1.

VOLUME X OCTOBER 1917.

Vol 27

Place	Date	Hour	Summary of Events and Information	Remarks and references to Appendices
ASCOT CAMP, WESTOUTRE	1.10.17	1.50pm	The Battalion left ASCOT CAMP and marched to BERTHEN area, arriving at 4pm.	
BERTHEN AREA	2.10.17	1.35pm	The Battalion left BERTHEN area and marched to MONT DES CATS arriving at 3pm.	
MONT DES CATS	3.10.17		Company training carried on. Weather wet.	
"	4.10.17		Weather wet.	
		3.30am	Received a message that the unit was to be ready to move off at 2 hours notice.	
"	5.10.17		Weather very wet.	
		5pm	Conference of Adjutants and Quartermasters at Brigade Headquarters. Companies fired on the range.	
"	6.10.17		Weather very wet.	
"	7.10.17		Weather very cold. Church Parades.	
"	8.10.17	9am	The Battalion moved from MONT DES CATS to ASCOT CAMP arriving at 10.30am.	

WAR DIARY
or
INTELLIGENCE SUMMARY. VOLUME X PAGE 2
(Erase heading not required.) OCTOBER 1917

Army Form C. 2118.

Place	Date	Hour	Summary of Events and Information	Remarks and references to Appendices
ASCOT CAMP WESTOUTRE	9.10.17	4 p.m.	The Battalion entrained at WESTOUTRE and arrived at SCOTTISH WOOD at 9.30 p.m.	
SCOTTISH WOOD	10.10.17		The Battalion left SCOTTISH WOOD and marched to front line relieving :-	
			1 Battalion H.A.C.	
			2 Companies R.W.F.	
			2 Battalions LEICESTER REGT.	
			Casualties :- 2/Lt A.G. SEEBORN wounded, wounded 33 o.r. missing 3 o.r.	
	11.10.17	8 a.m.	Relief complete	
			Dispositions - CHELUVELT HQ BUTTE J.10.a.7.8.	
			Battalion H.Q BUTTE J.11.c.6.3. to J.11.c.35.50.	
			A Company J.11.a.1.3. to J.11.c.6.3.	
			B " J.11.c.35.50. to J.11.c.6.3.	
			C " J.11.c.35.50. to J.11.c.0.2.	
			D " J.11.c.50.35. to J.11.c.6.7.	

Army Form C. 2118.

WAR DIARY
or
INTELLIGENCE SUMMARY.
(Erase heading not required.)

VOLUME X PAGE 3
OCTOBER 1917.

Place	Date	Hour	Summary of Events and Information	Remarks and references to Appendices
	11.10.17		Con:td.	
			Enemy shelled support line and Battalion Headquarters heavily and considerably all day.	
			Casualties :- Wounded - Lt. S.C. WITHERSPOON and 2/Lt o.R.	
	12.10.17	5.30p.m.	Battalion Headquarters moved to J.10.c.6.3.	
			Enemy artillery very active all night.	
			Casualties :- Killed in action 2/Lt. C. HANDS and 4 o.R.	
			Wounded 15 o.R.	
	13.10.17		The 11th N.F. relieved the Battalion in the front line. Relief complete 8 am.	
			B & D. Companies remained in support to 11th N.F. at J.10.d.0.5.	
			H.Qrs. and A and C. Companies withdrew to the BUND	
			Casualties :- Killed 1 o.R. Wounded 5 o.R.	
BUND	14.10.17		The Battalion less B & D. Companies, was relieved by the 8th YORKS and withdrew to camp at N.2.B.2.7.	

Army Form C. 2118.

PAGE 9

VOLUME X

OCTOBER 1917

WAR DIARY
or
INTELLIGENCE SUMMARY.
(Erase heading not required.)

Place	Date	Hour	Summary of Events and Information	Remarks and references to Appendices
	14.10.17		Cont'd.	
			Casualties:- Killed 2 o.r., Wounded 6 o.r.	
N.2.6.2.7.	15.10.17		Enemy aircraft very busy at night dropping bombs on DICKEBUSCH.	
			Casualties:- Wounded 2 o.r.	
- " -	16.10.17	7 pm	B & D Companies relieved by 2 companies of 8th YORKS and withdrew to the BUND.	
			Enemy aircraft active day & night.	
			The G.O.C. Division presented medals to the following:-	
			Bar to M.M.:- 15952 Pte A. Constantine	
			Military Medal:- 19348 Sgt W. Powell, 18483 Sgt W. Sledge,	
			52840 Sgt A. Burns, 18050 Sgt E. Wilkinson, 15524 Cpl J.H. Pattison,	
			35327 Cpl J. Ensinelli, 2114 Sgt J. Robson, 28892 L/Cpl J. Roy,	
			16744 Pte D. Pattison, 52868 Pte J. Cornthwaite, 18168 Pte E.C. Smith,	
			302645 Pte J.W. Howlett, 301505 Pte G. Kempster, 52944 Pte A. Shaw,	
			25193 Pte J. Byrne, 17024 Pte J.J. Henderson, 10104 Pte J.J. Woodruff.	

Army Form C. 2118.

WAR DIARY
INTELLIGENCE SUMMARY.
(Erase heading not required.)

Volume X   Page 5
October 1917

Place	Date	Hour	Summary of Events and Information	Remarks and references to Appendices
	16.10.17		Con'd.	
			21024 L/Cpl J.O. Dean, 28478 Cpl R. Walton, 1696 Sgt F. Sallivant, 28803 Cpl J. Anderson, 17417 Cpl E.W. Jefferson, 38557 Pte G.S. Rowell, 21909 L/Cpl J. McKenna, 24772 L/Cpl J. Bowman, 1713 Pte W. Webster, 46070 Pte A. Luck, 201353 Pte J. Simm, 46948 Pte J.L. Holt, 582 Pte E. Hodges, 45984 Pte W. Howe, 202205 Pte J. Bowman, 18124 Cpl W. Thompson.	
N.2.6.2.7.	17.10.17	1 p.m.	H.Qrs, A and C Companies left DICKEBUSCH and marched to RAILWAY DUGOUTS arriving at 3 p.m. Enemy fired a few shells into the BUND area during the night.	
RAILWAY DUGOUTS	18.10.17	3 p.m.	The Battalion left RAILWAY DUGOUTS and proceeded to front line near REUTEL relieving the 8th YORKS. The enemy shelled our area very heavily all night. Casualties:- Wounded & gassed 2/Lt J.P. Carroll, Killed 6 o.r., Wounded 11 o.r.	

Army Form C. 2118.

PAGE 6

WAR DIARY
or
INTELLIGENCE SUMMARY.

VOLUME X OCTOBER 1917

(Erase heading not required.)

Place	Date	Hour	Summary of Events and Information	Remarks and references to Appendices
	19.10.17	6.30am	Relief complete	
			Dispositions :-	
			H.Qrs & Aid Post J.10.c.6.3.	
			A Company J.11.c.6.3 - J.10.a.7.8.	
			B " J.11.d.1.3 - J.11.c.6.3.	
			C " J.11.c.35.50 - J.11.c.0.2.	
			D " J.11.c.50.35 - J.11.c.6.7.	
			Enemy shelled the area intermittently all day and night, Battalion H.Q. receiving special attention. A few gas shells were also fired by the enemy about J.11.c.6.3. Enemy snipers active.	
			Casualties :- Killed 3 o.r., Wounded 3 o.r.	
	20.10.17		Intermittent shelling of our forward area east of POLYGON WOOD, POLYGON BEKE receiving special attention. Enemy snipers less active.	
			Enemy aircraft again flew low over our lines at dawn.	

WAR DIARY
or
INTELLIGENCE SUMMARY.

Army Form C. 2118.

VOLUME X PAGE 7
OCTOBER 1917

Place	Date	Hour	Summary of Events and Information	Remarks and references to Appendices
	20-10-17		Cont'd.	
			and dusk they were engaged by Lewis guns. Casualties:- Killed 5 O.R., wounded 12 O.R.	
	21-10-17		Fairly quiet during the day.	
		5 p.m.	An S.O.S. was put up by an aeroplane and left, a small party of the enemy was seen near JUDGE COPSE, the party was fired upon by a Lewis gun and dispersed. The enemy shelled heavily in the evening. The Battalion was relieved by the 9th K.O.Y.L.I. 21st Division. Casualties:- Killed 13 O.R., wounded 13 O.R.	
	22-10-17	8 a.m.	Relief complete; the Battalion withdrew to the BUND. Battalion left the BUND and embussed at KRUISSTRAATHOEK	
		10 a.m.	at 2 p.m. arriving at TATINGHEM at 7 p.m.	
TATINGHEM	23-10-17		The day was spent cleaning up.	
" "	24-10-17		Weather wet.	
" "	25-10-17		The G.O.C. Brigade inspected Battalion in the morning	

WAR DIARY
or
INTELLIGENCE SUMMARY.
(Erase heading not required.)

Army Form C. 2118.
PAGE 8
VOLUME X
OCTOBER 1917

Place	Date	Hour	Summary of Events and Information	Remarks and references to Appendices
	25.10.17		The G.O.C. Division presented ribbons to the following :-	
			2/Lt. T/Capt. E. GRAY D.S.O., LIEUT R.S.F. MITCHELL M.C.	
			2/LIEUT W.J. ARRIS M.C., 2/LIEUT W.T. CALDWELL M.C.	
			" F.E.C.D. SMITH M.C. " G.C. WRIGHT M.C.	
			16101 Sgt. R. COWELL D.C.M., 45960 Sgt. R. Minehardo D.C.M.	
			32329 " G.W. JACKSON D.C.M. 15384 Corp J. Bellerby Bar to M.M.	
			REV. E.G. WELLS M.C. MAJOR E. BORROW D.S.O.	
			2/LIEUT J.D. INCHES reported his arrival posted to D. Coy.	
			" J.S. WILSON reported his arrival posted to A. Coy.	
TATINGHEM	26.10.17		Weather :- Very wet	
			Companies were unable to carry out any training	
"	27.10.17		The Battalion fired on "C" range Q. 29.C.	
"	28.10.17		Church Parade	
"	29.10.17	10.15am	The G.O.C. Brigade inspected the Brigade and presented	
			chits of Valour to the following :-	
			CAPT. L.M. GREENWOOD M.C. 2/LIEUT J.P. CARROLL	

Army Form C. 2118.

PAGE 9

WAR DIARY
or
INTELLIGENCE SUMMARY.
(Erase heading not required.)

VOLUME X
OCTOBER 1917

Place	Date	Hour	Summary of Events and Information	Remarks and references to Appendices
	29.10.17		Cont'd.	
			2/Lieut S.F. Johnston, 2/Lieut W.C. Hodgson,	
			2/Lieut I. Bewley.	
			Sgt E. Ratcliffe, Sgt J.K. Waldram, Sgt J.S. Hammond,	
			Sgt J. Lawson, Corpl J.R. Robson, L/Corpl J.Y. Bowman,	
			L/Corpl E. Mitchell, Pte J. Carr, Pte S. Towks, Pte J.E. Miller,	
			Pte J. Angus, Pte E. Guinan, Pte E.T. Wilson, Pte J.B. Reed,	
			Pte G. Killen, Pte J. Yates, Pte W. Wilkinson, Pte J. Armstrong.	
TATINGHEM	30.10.17		Owing to wet weather training was cancelled.	
"	31.10.17		The Commander-in-Chief inspected the Brigade, and	
			expressed his Satisfaction with the troops.	

E. Gray, Captain
Comdg. 18th (Serv.) Bn. DURHAM LT. INFTY.